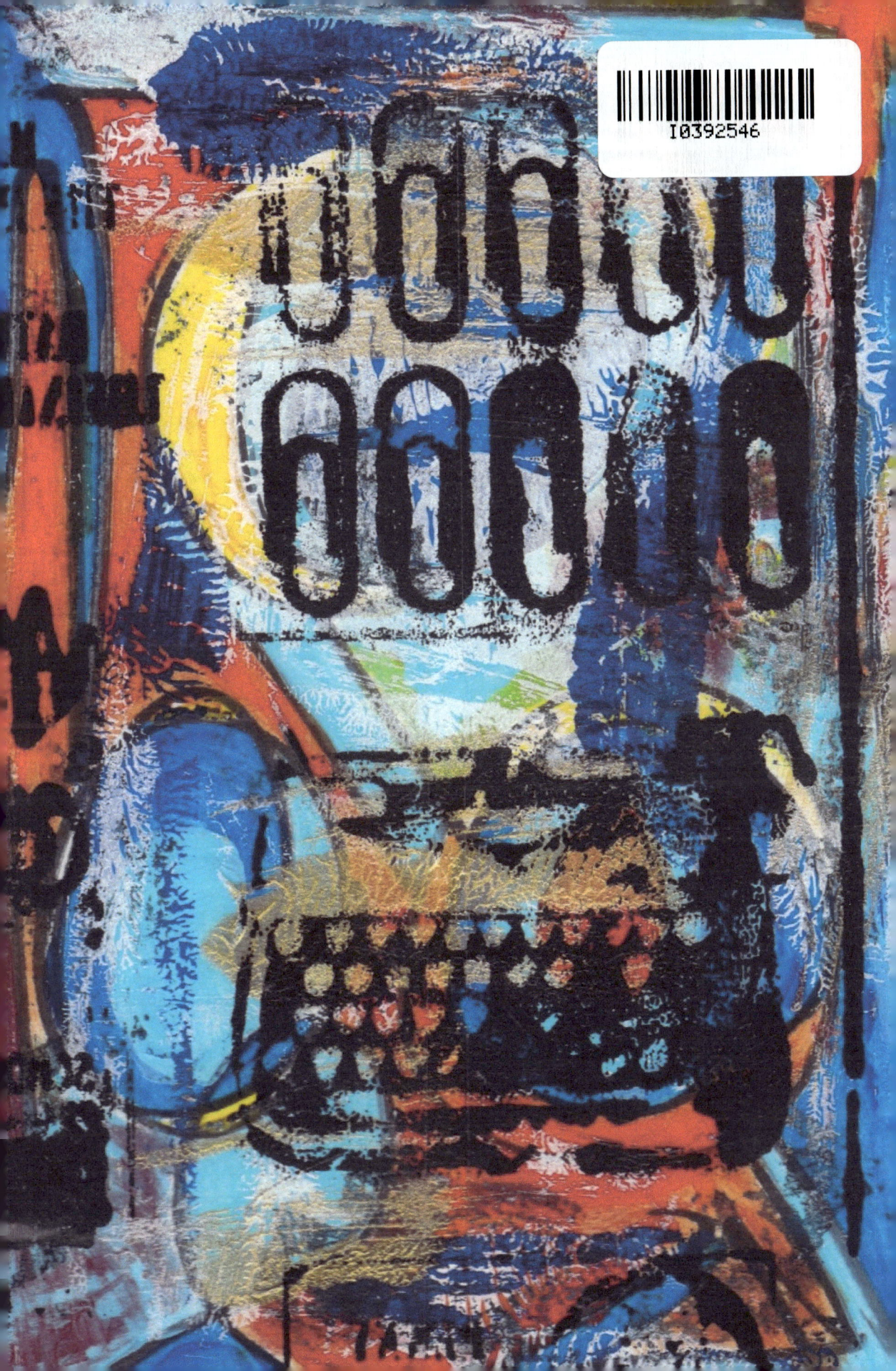

MAIL ART OPEN CALL

NO JURY
NO THEME
NO RETURNS
NO GUIDELINES
OPEN TO ALL
FREE
NO DEADLINES

Quarterly Paperback and E-Book

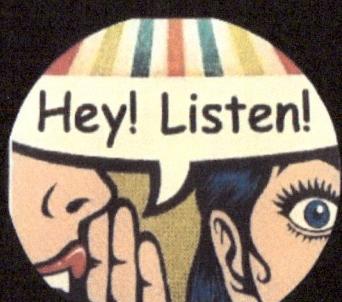

ALL Work will be shown on theintrovertedpost.com
ALL Work will be published in an e-book and paperback.
The e-book will be available for download for free the first 5 days of publication.
If you leave an instagram @ on the work I will tag your account when posting.

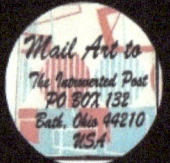

Send Art To:

The Introverted Post
PO BOX 132
Bath, OHIO 44210
USA

All sales of the paperback will be used towards,
Reciprocating Art back to anyone leaving a return
address and running The Introverted Post.

Quarterly Book
Published
January 31
April 30
July 31
October 31

Deadlines are one month before publish date for each Vol.

The Introverted Post reserves the right to exclude erotica, hate, and anything that wouldn't pass a fair use test.

MAILART

gaglione

gaglion

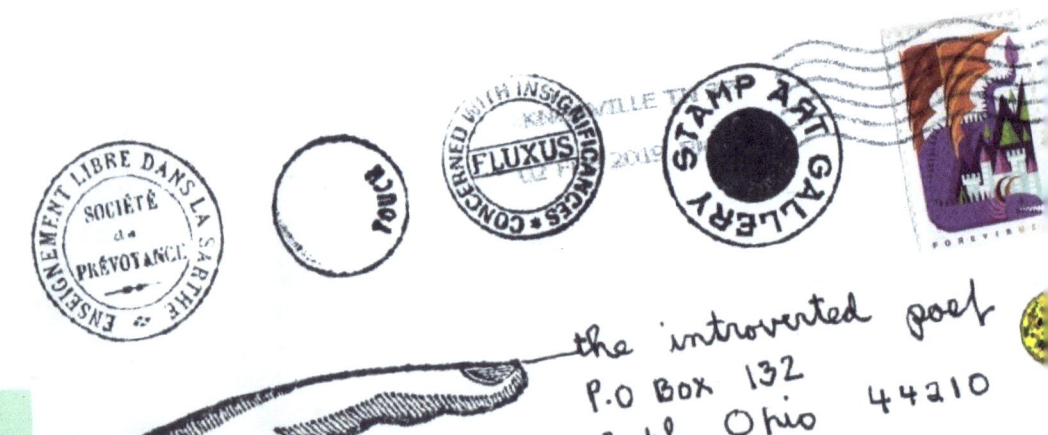

SOCIÉTÉ de PRÉVOTANCE
ENSEIGNEMENT LIBRE DANS LA SARTHE

TOUT

CONCERNED WITH INSIGNIFICANCE — FLUXUS — KNOWLEDGEVILLE TEMP 02 2019

STAMP ART GALLERY

FOREVER

ORIGINAL

gaglione

the introverted poet
P.O BOX 132
Bath Ohio 44210

First Class

44210-013232

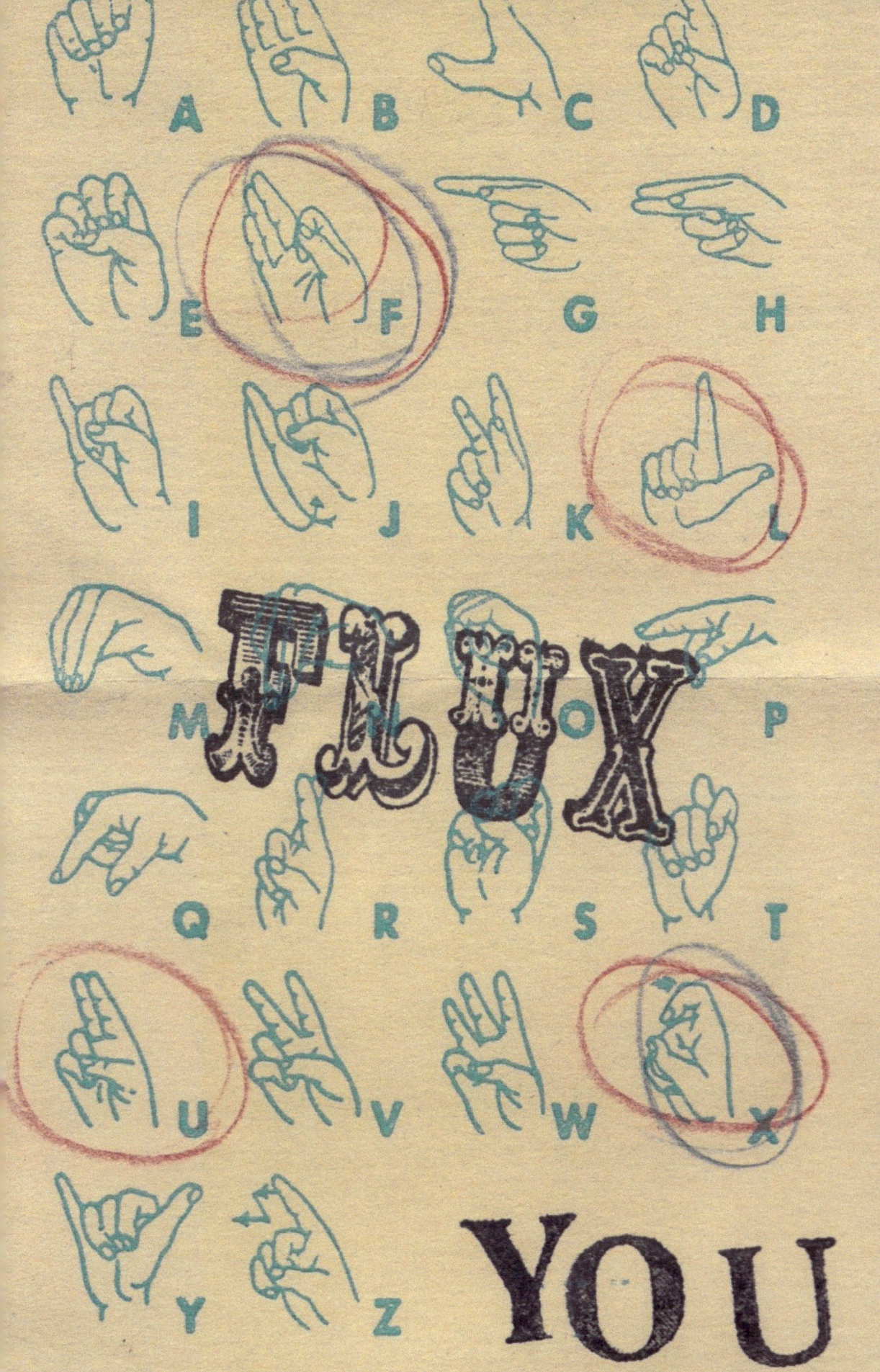

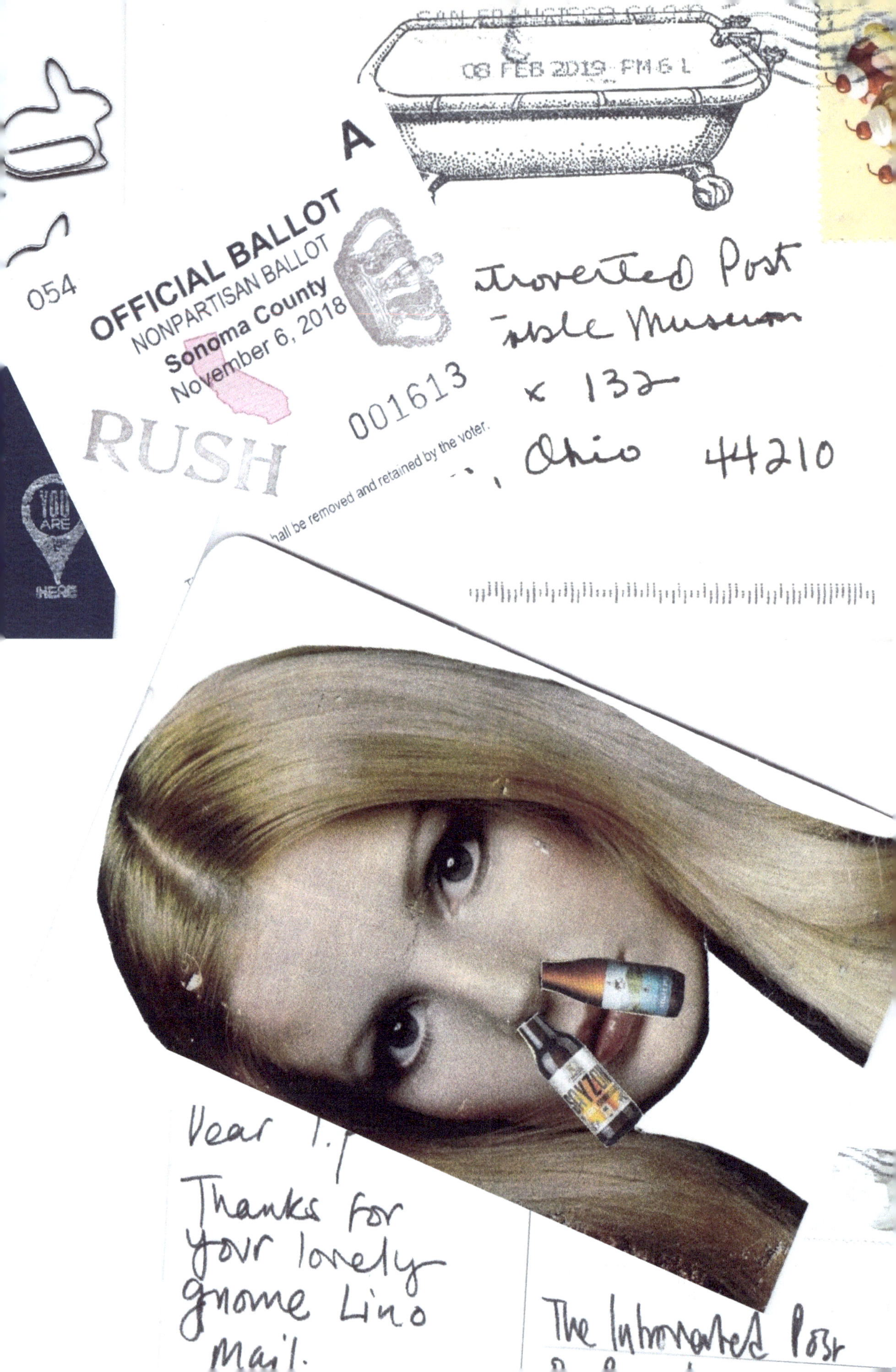

054

08 FEB 2019 PM 6 L

OFFICIAL BALLOT
NONPARTISAN BALLOT
Sonoma County
November 6, 2018

A

RUSH

001613

hall be removed and retained by the voter.

troverted Post
-sble Museum
x 132
, Ohio 44210

Dear T.T

Thanks for
your lonely
gnome Lino
Mail.

The Intronerted Post

that tap tap tapping can it be?
I dare say why not. maybe
maybe-if I put my heart in just
the right position and whisper into
the moonlight. yes. yes. you're right
dreams do come true. Lenore Lenore
nevermore never more...

...ANT CHILDREN

...and arresting passengers on Greyhound buses. De...
...orrific abuses unleashed by the Trump administrat...

...ds of pages of evidence documenting U.S. Customs and Border...
...d verbally abusing *children*. The majority of these children are...
America. Some are teenage mothers. Some are escaping gang v...

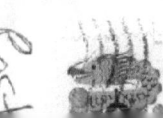
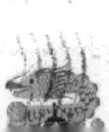
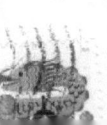

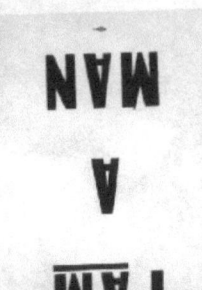
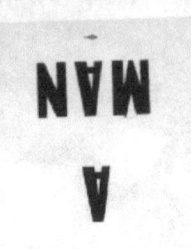
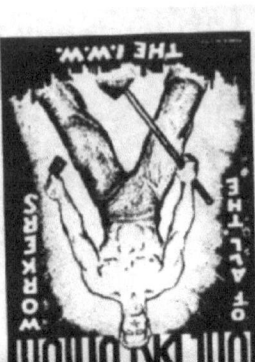
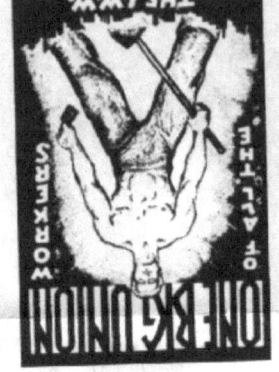
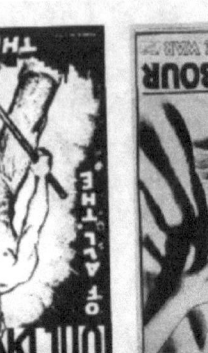
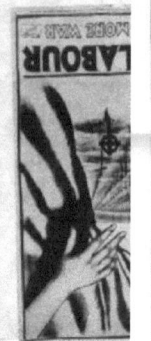
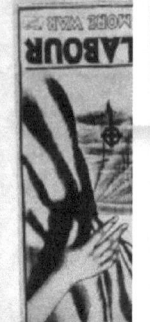
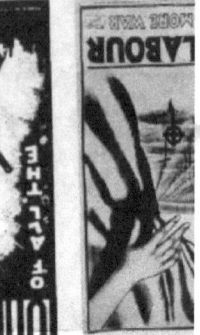

MAN
I AM A MAN

THE I.W.W.
ONE BIG UNION
OF ALL THE WORKERS

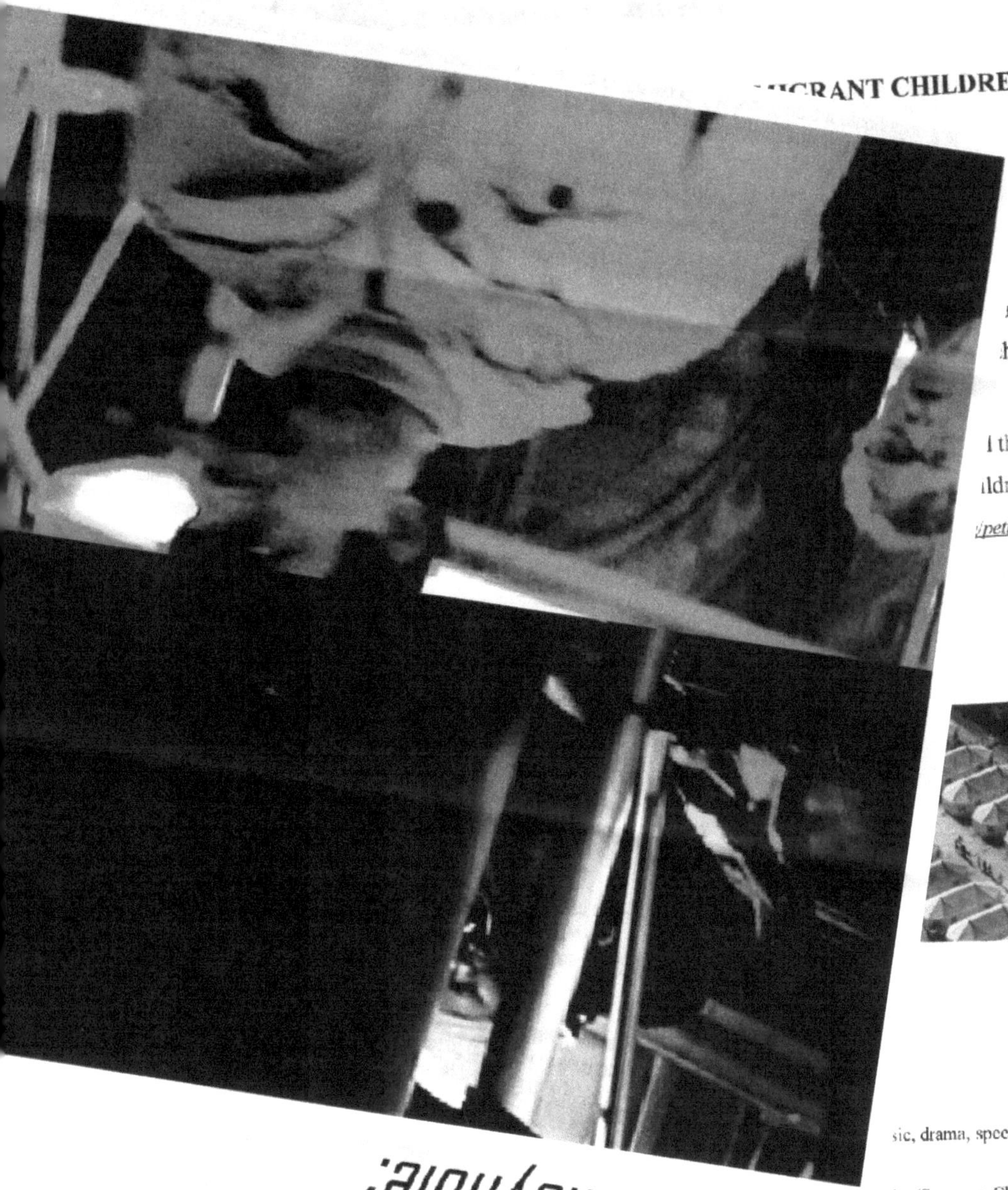

LABOUR

ech: *Second Thoughts on the First Amendment* from the book *Declarations of Independence* by Howard Zinn.

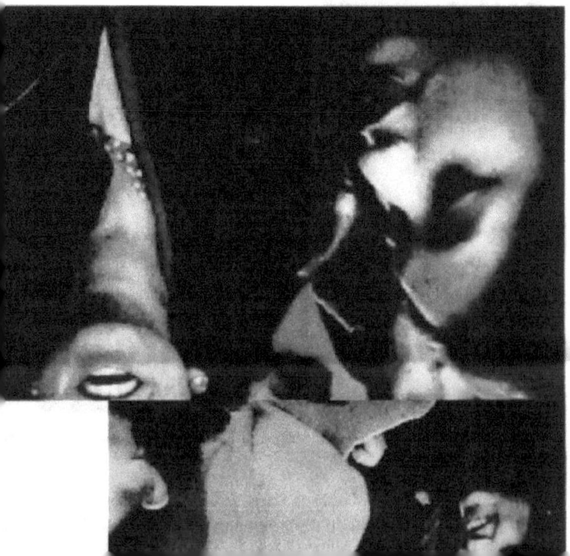

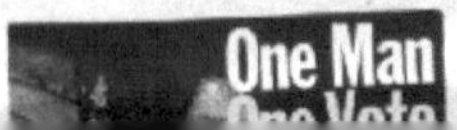

d powerful. It was just part of ... of hundreds of thousands of people all over

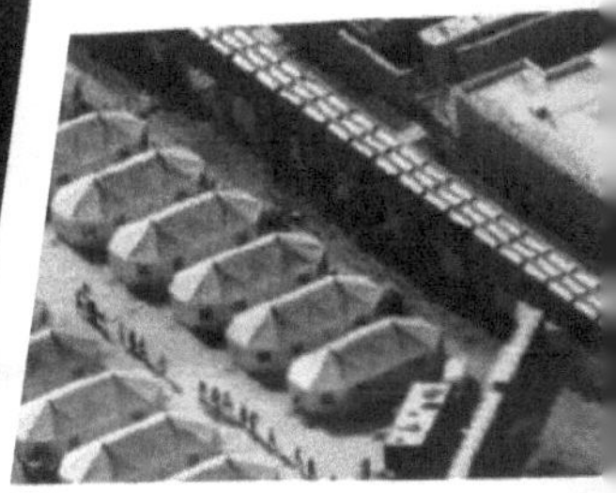

king to millions of people in many different ways, bringing life to the First

an end to a war.

alice and keyhole:

ble design and eight large words printed on it:

tist (Seymour Chwast) turned his talents to

sic, drama, speech, demonstrative action,

petition/cbp-stop-abusing-child-

ildren in his agency's

l the Commissioner of

hildren are asylum seeke

nd Border Protection

mistration's anti-

s, Detaining asylum

RANT CHILDREN

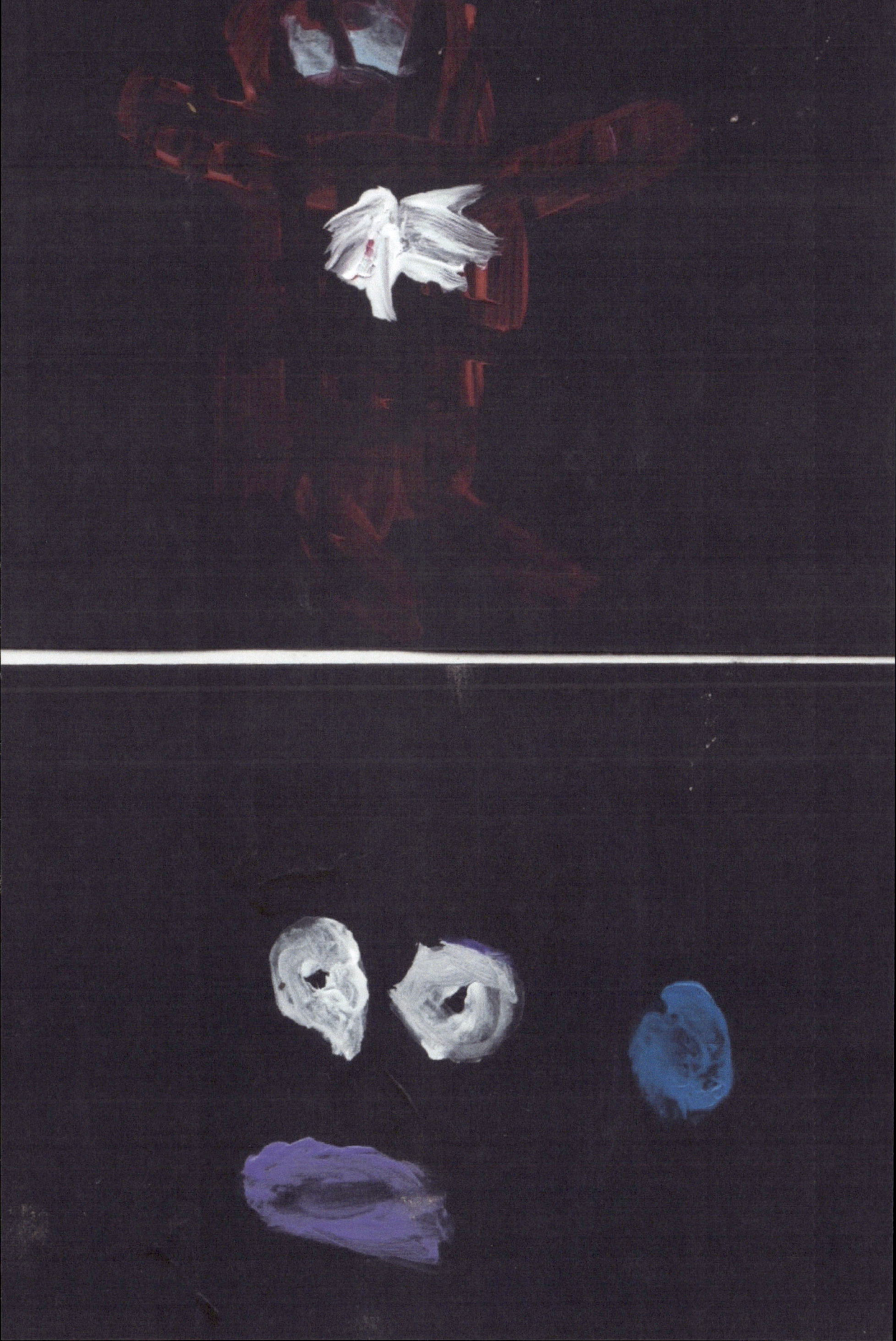

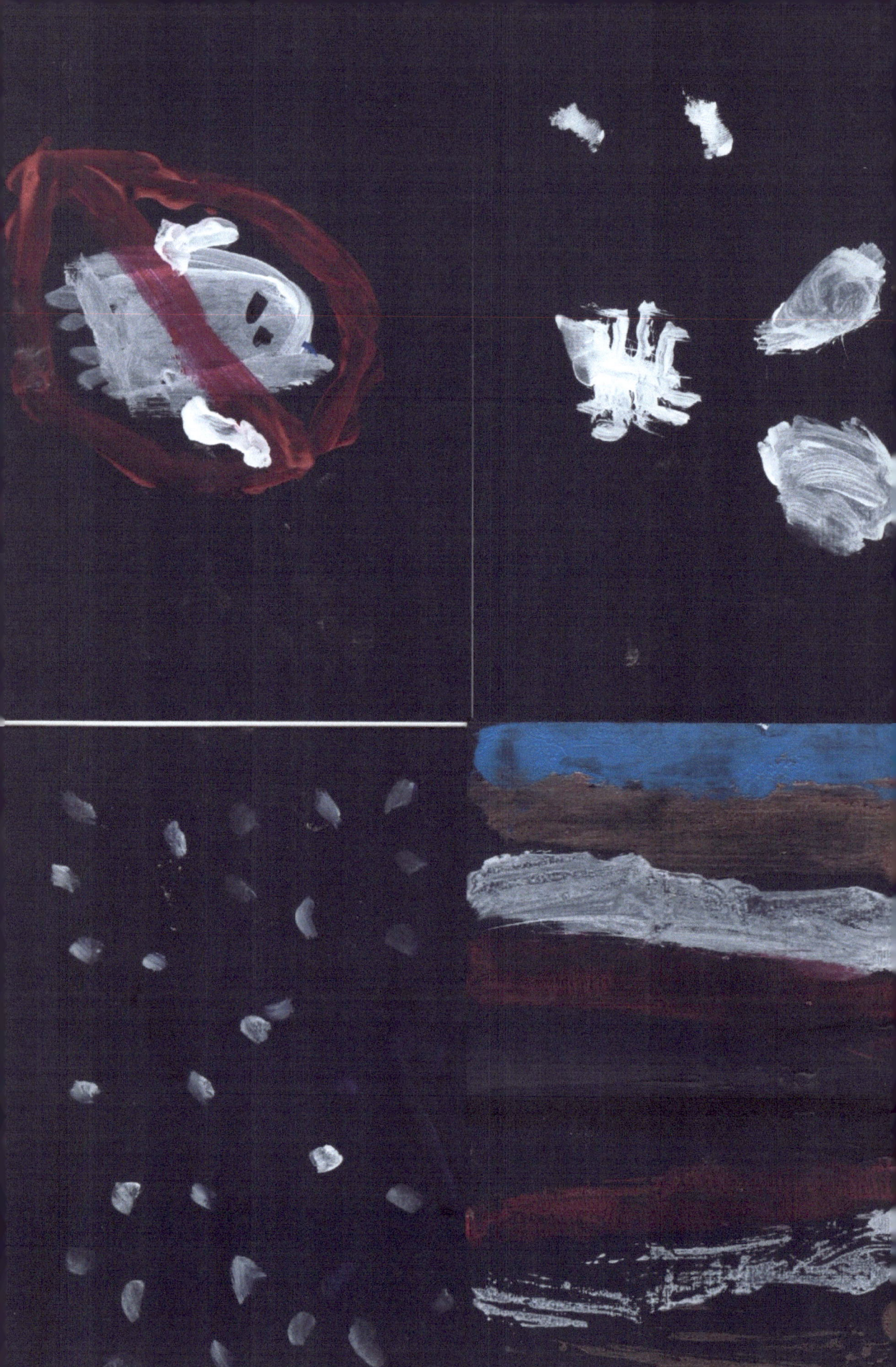

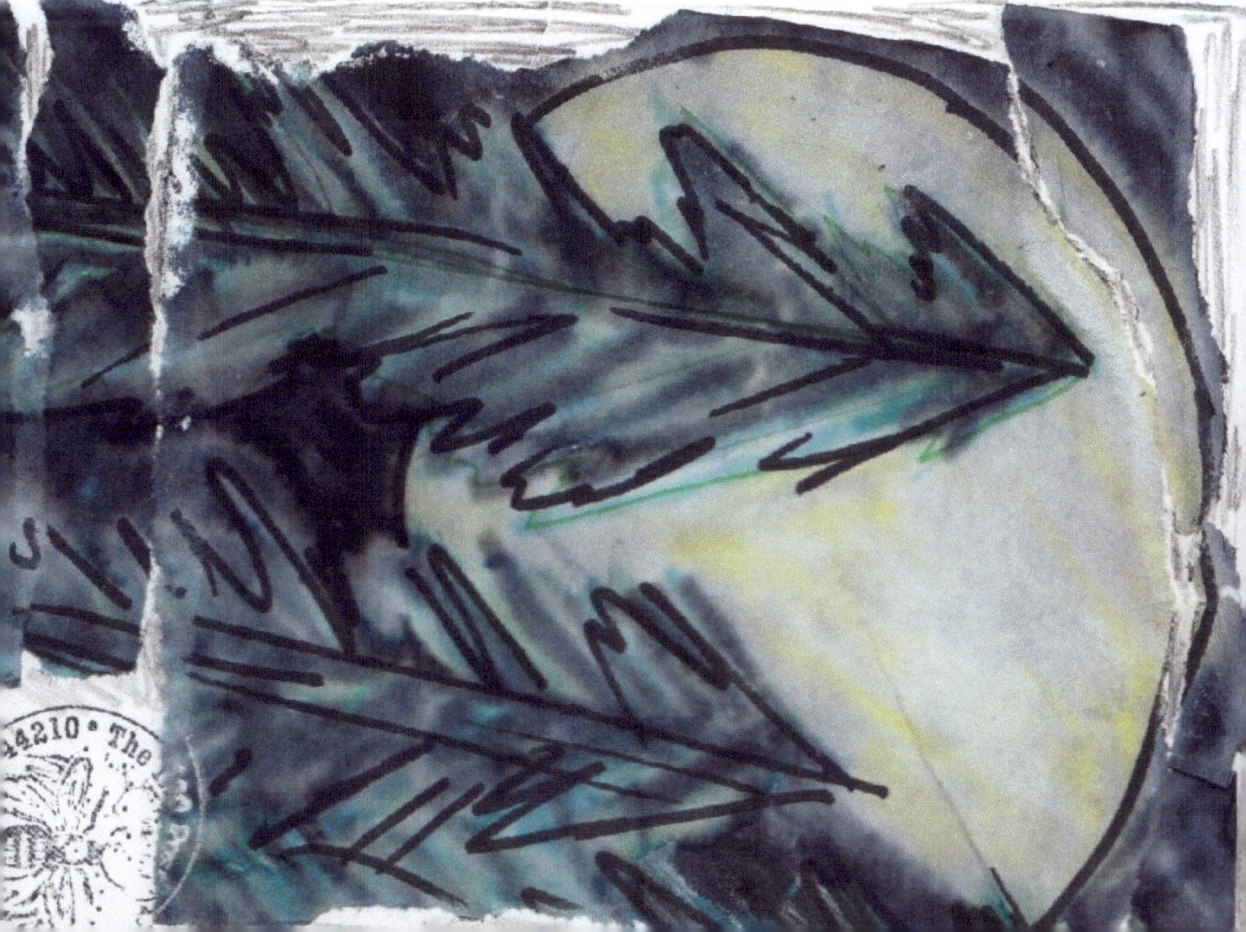

Nod to "The Snail" 2019

Gayne

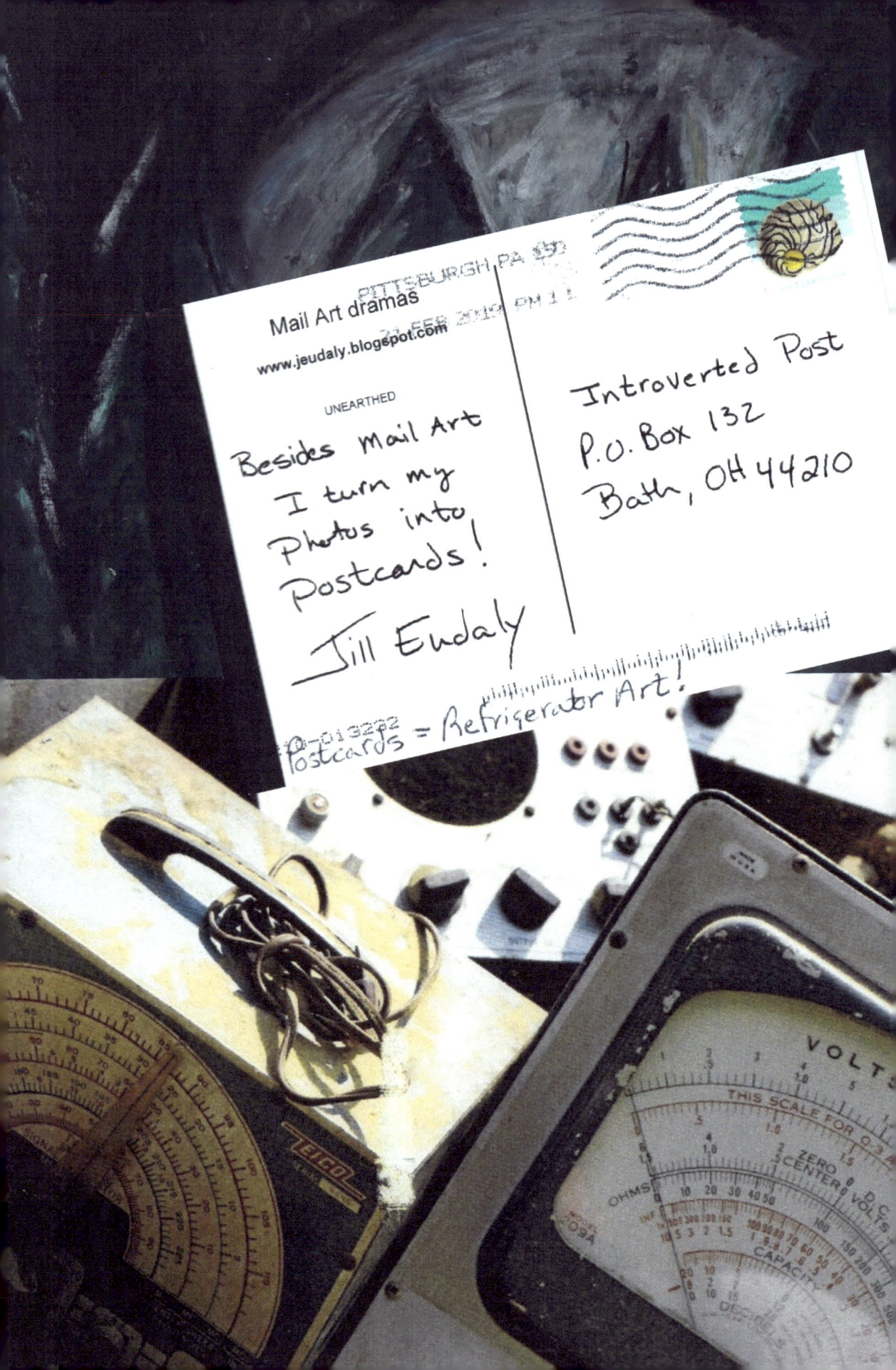

Mail Art dramas
www.jeudaly.blogspot.com

PITTSBURGH PA
21 FEB 2019 PM 1 L

UNEARTHED

Besides Mail Art
I turn my
Photos into
Postcards!

Jill Eudaly

Introverted Post
P.O. Box 132
Bath, OH 44210

Postcards = Refrigerator Art!

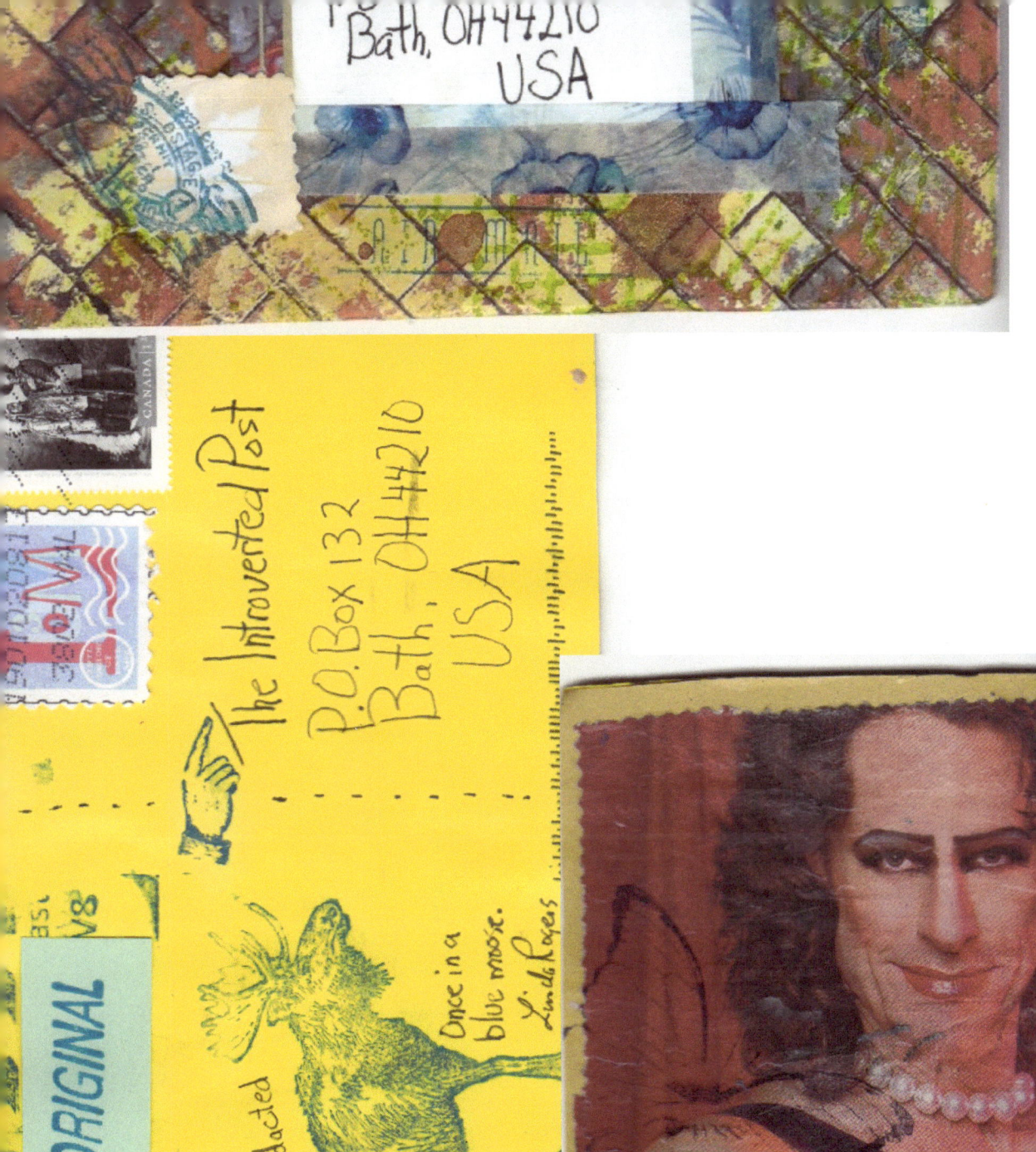

Bath, OH 44210
USA

The Introverted Post
P.O. Box 132
Bath, OH 44210
USA

ORIGINAL

Un-redacted

Once in a
blue moose.
Linda Rogers

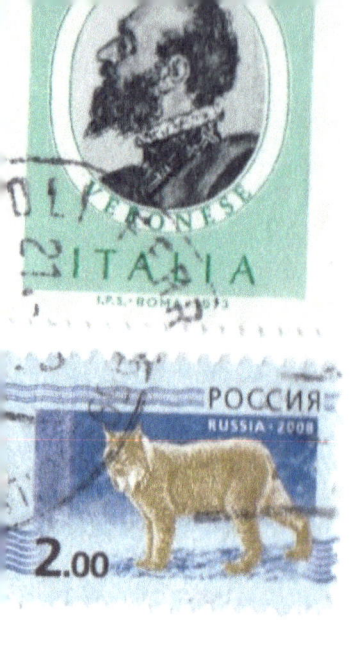
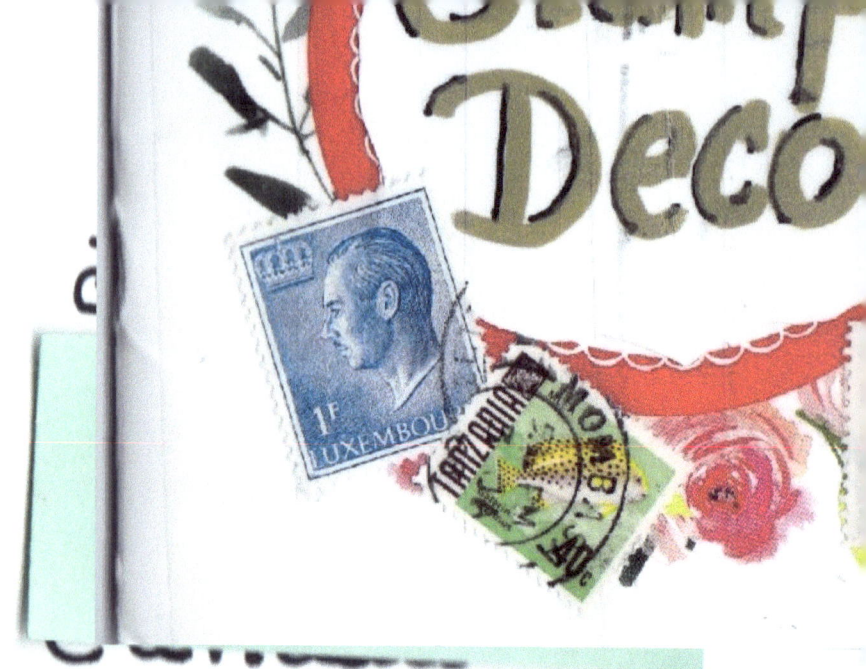

Stamp Deco

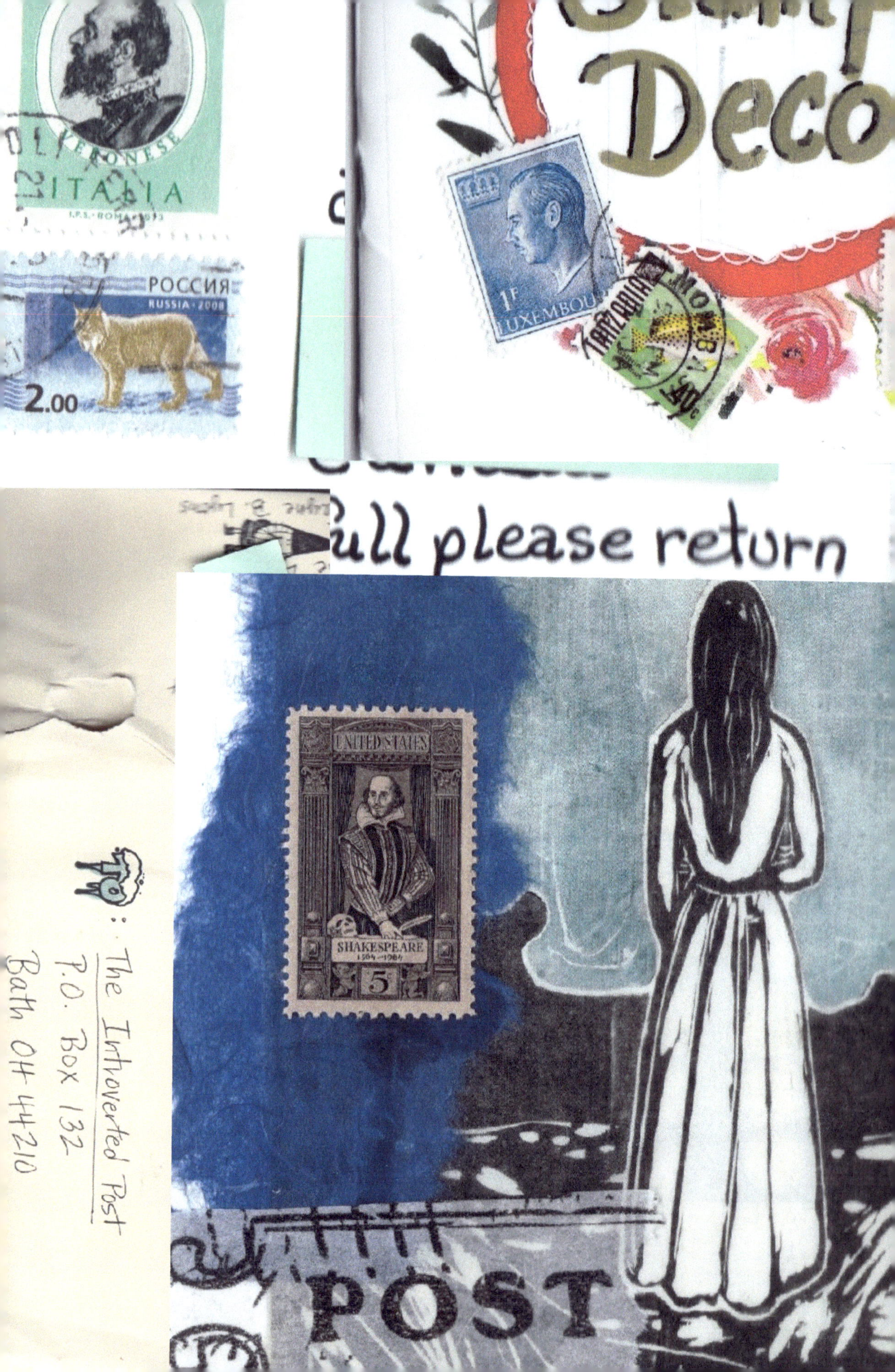

ull please return

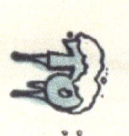

To: The Introverted Post
P.O. Box 132
Bath OH 44210

SHAKESPEARE
1564-1964
UNITED STATES
5¢

POST

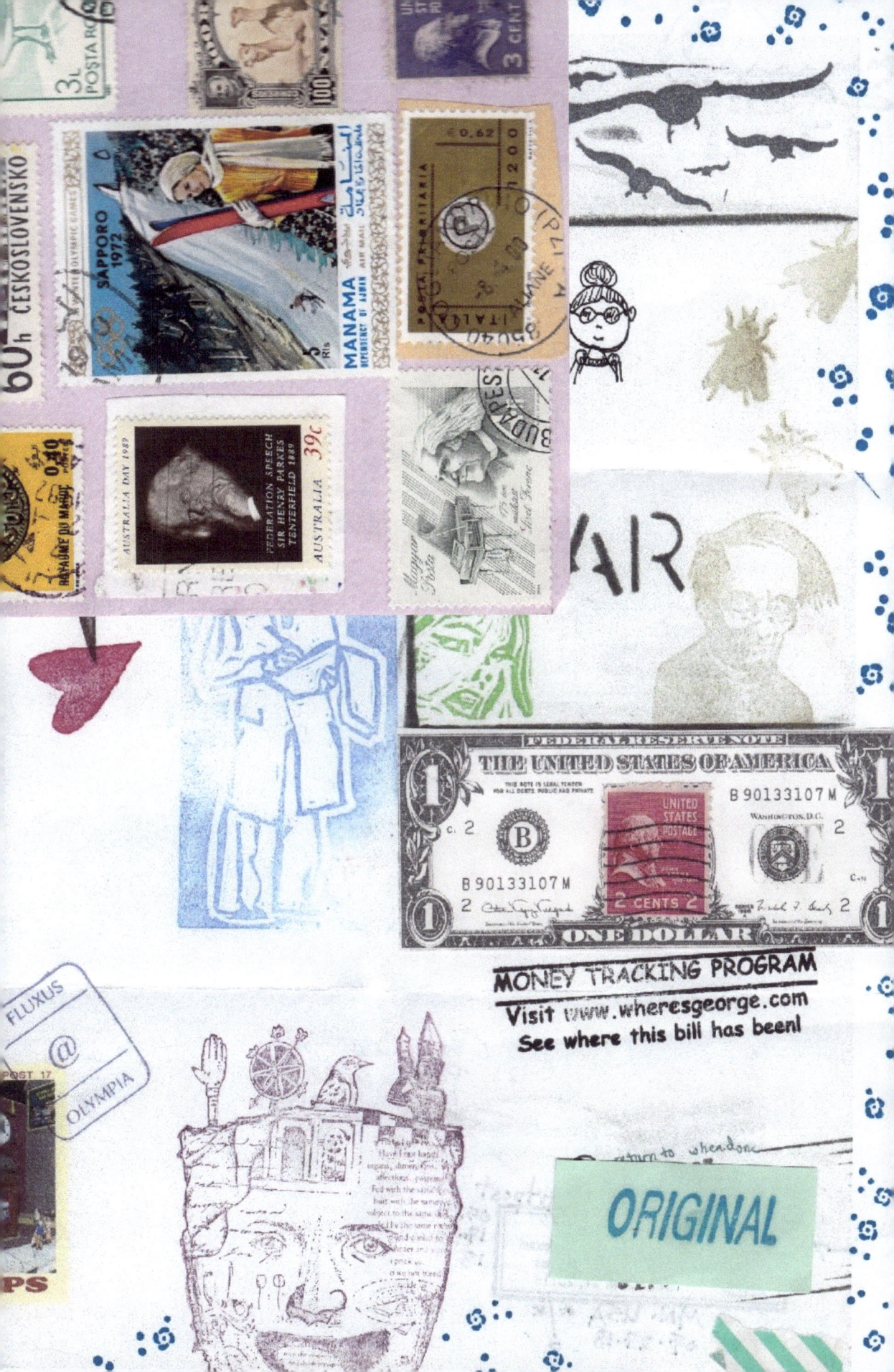

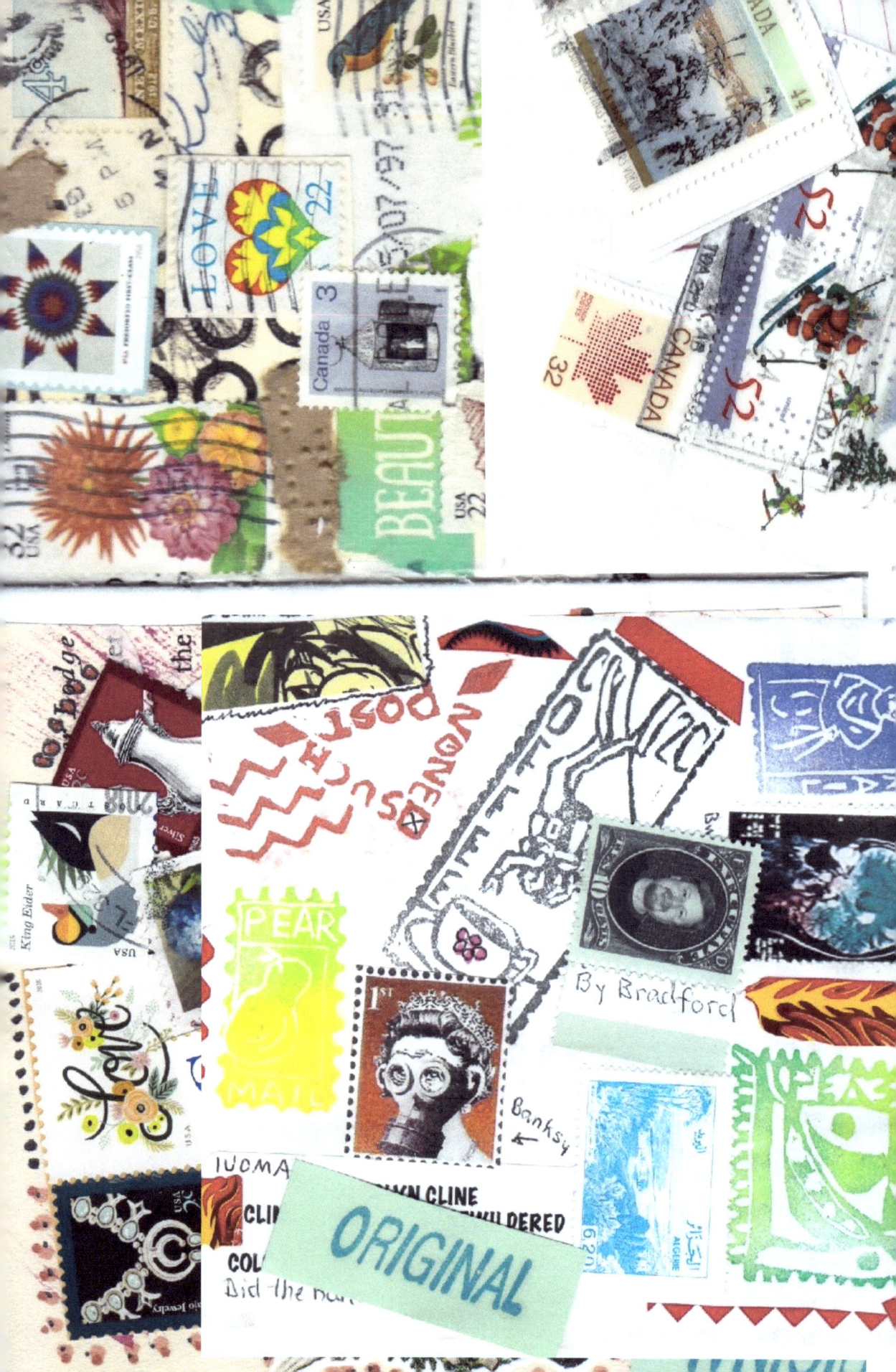

Ed Gieter ☮ USA

THIS STAMP'S 4-U

LYSERGIC

But the novel is not o[nly]
about contact between humans and extraterrestria[l]
it is also about contact, down here on Earth, with ea[ch]
other and with ourselves.

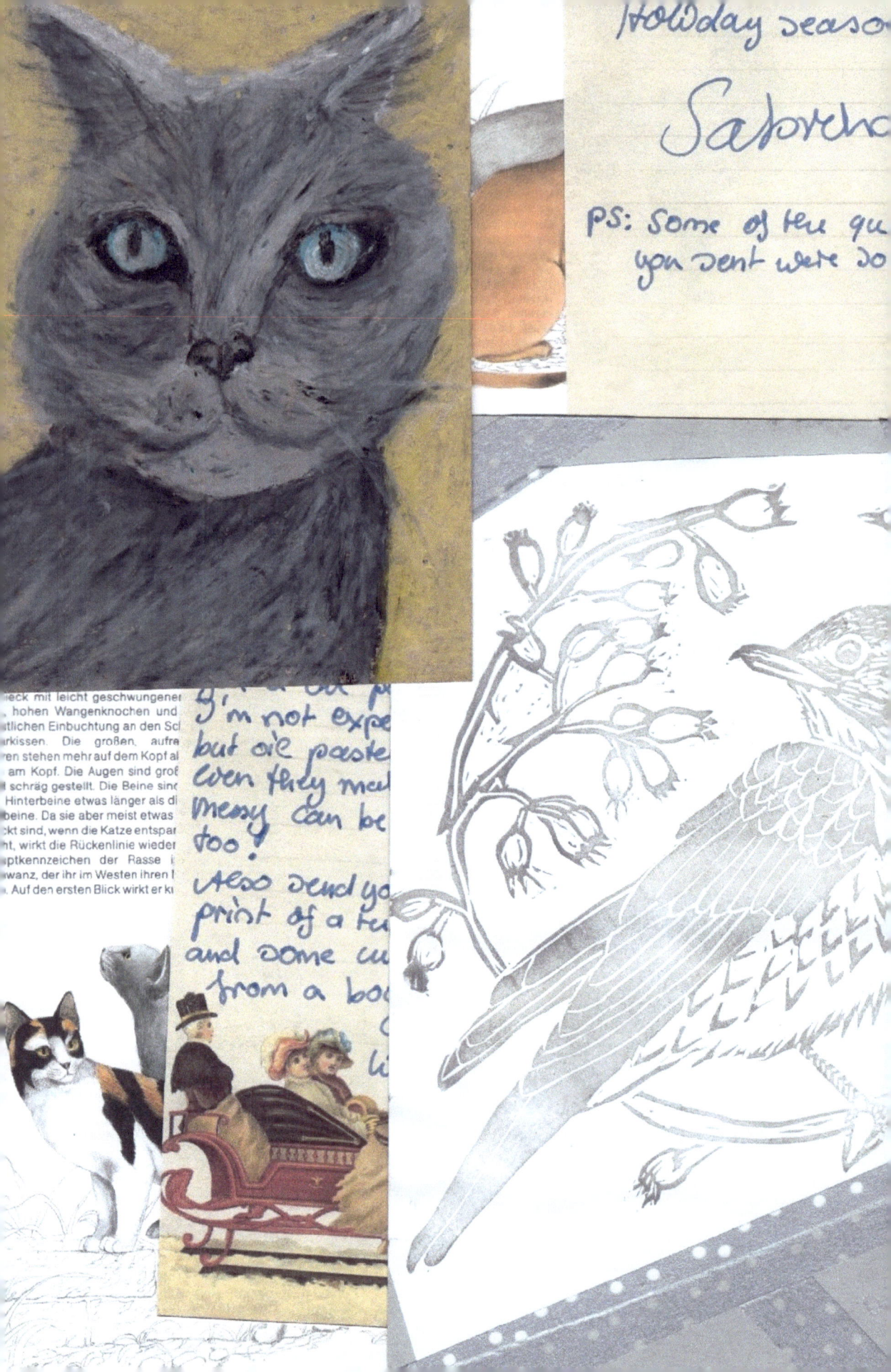

Holiday season

Satorcha

PS: Some of the qu
you sent were so

I'm not expe
but oie paste
wen they me
messy can be
too!

Also send yo
print of a tu
and some cu
from a boo
li

eck mit leicht geschwungener
, hohen Wangenknochen und
stlichen Einbuchtung an den Sc
rkissen. Die großen, aufra
ren stehen mehr auf dem Kopf al
am Kopf. Die Augen sind groß
l schräg gestellt. Die Beine sind
Hinterbeine etwas länger als di
beine. Da sie aber meist etwas
ckt sind, wenn die Katze entspar
ht, wirkt die Rückenlinie wieder
ptkennzeichen der Rasse i
wanz, der ihr im Westen ihren
. Auf den ersten Blick wirkt er k

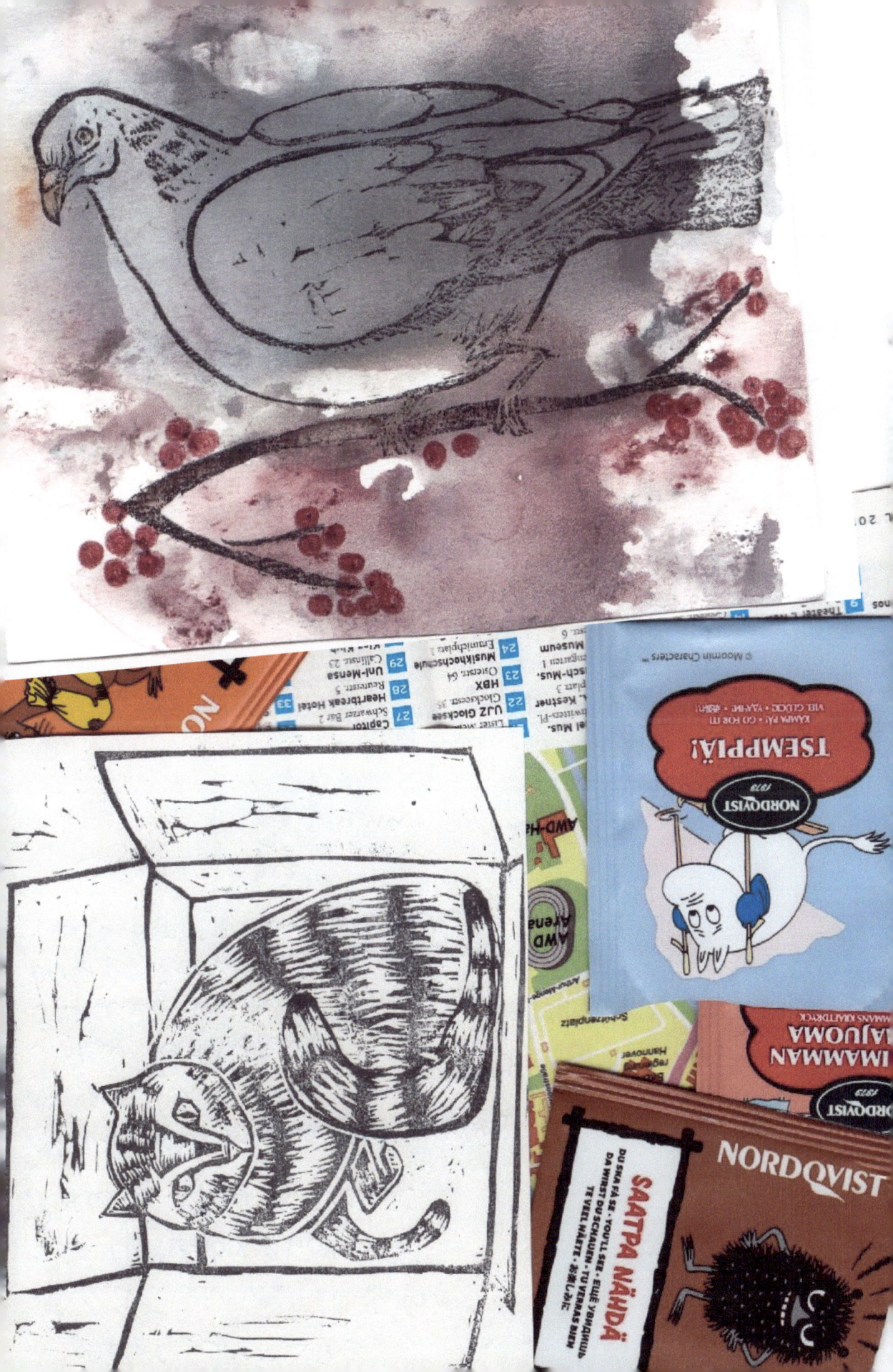

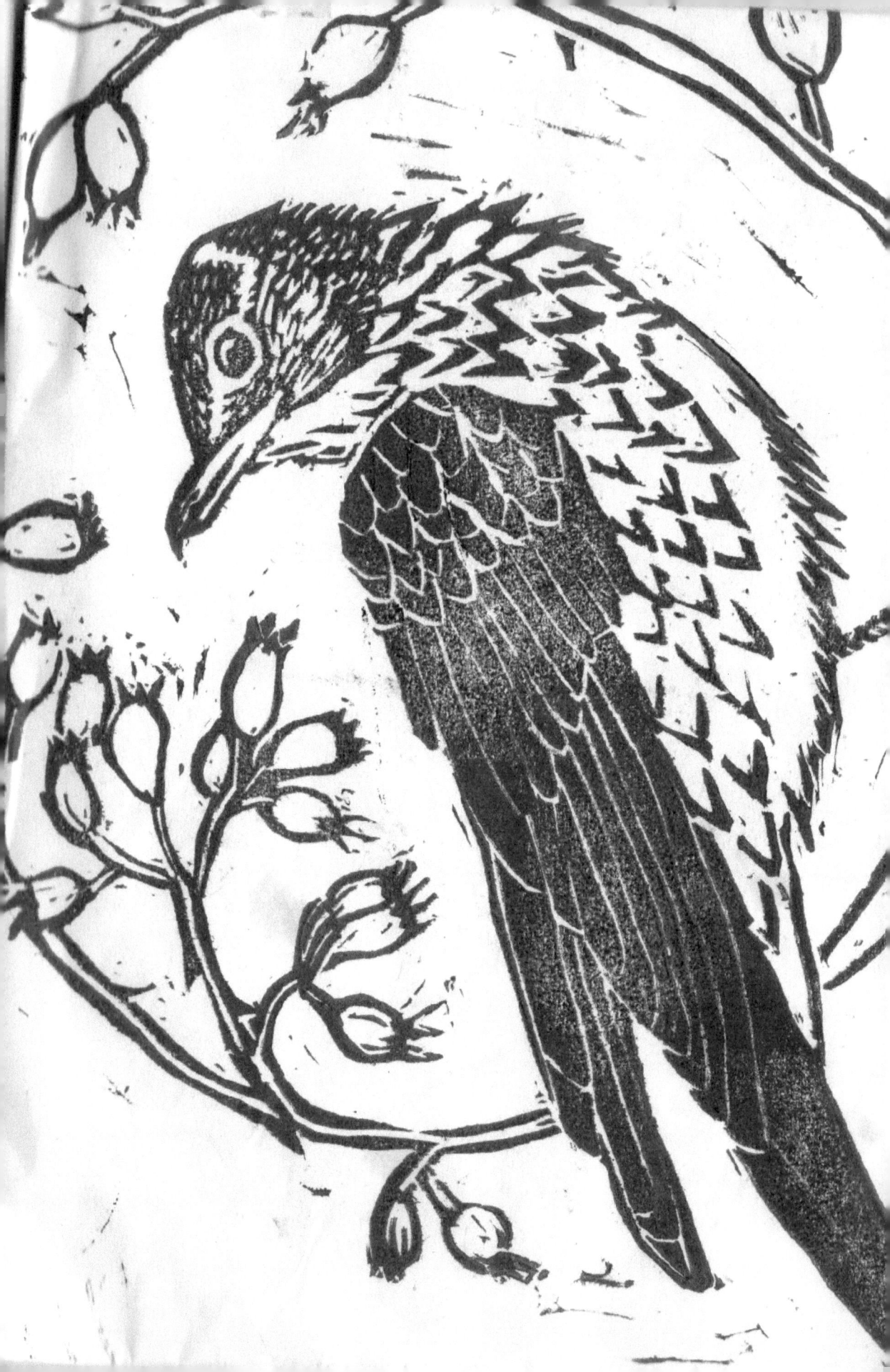

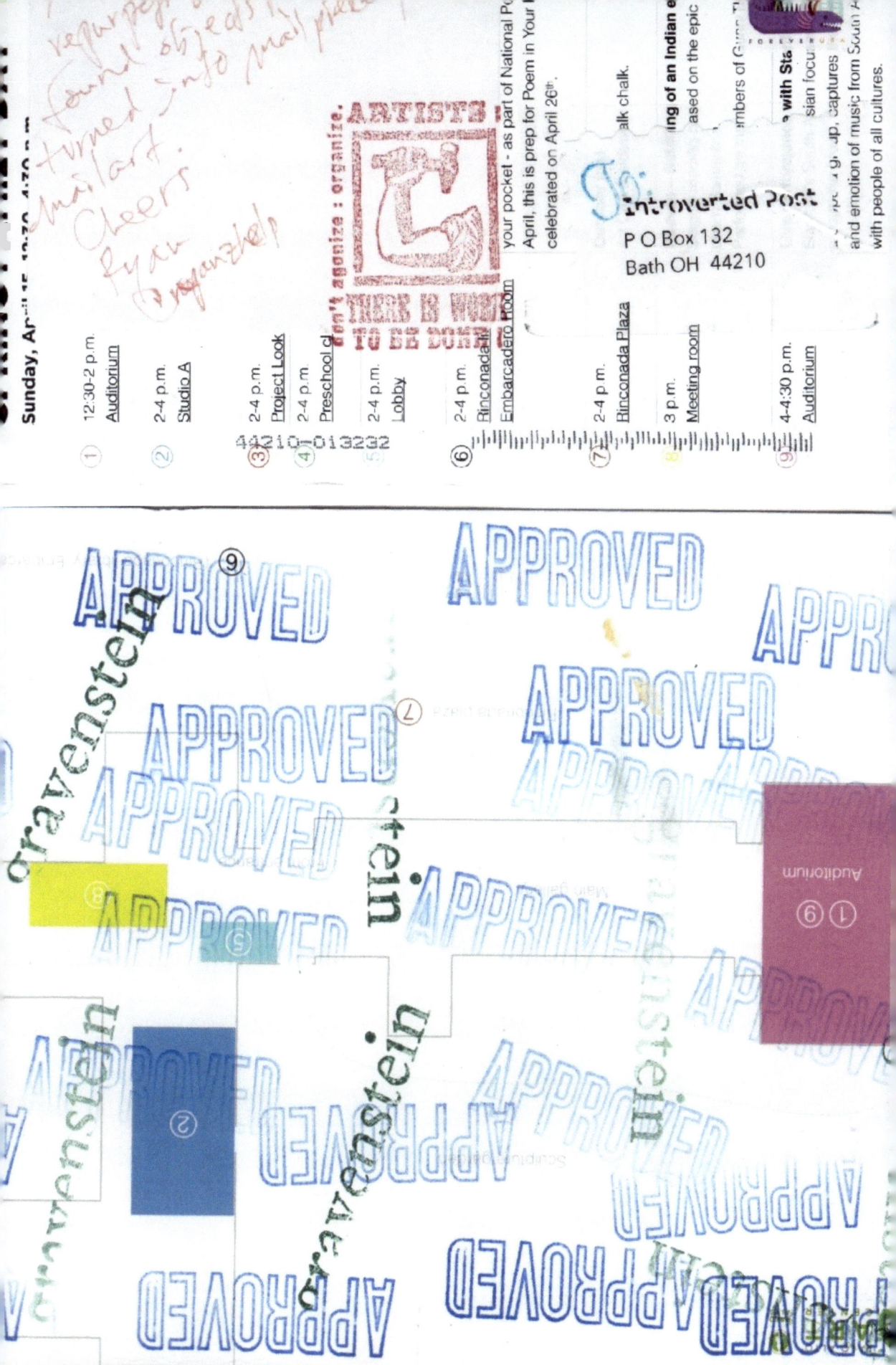

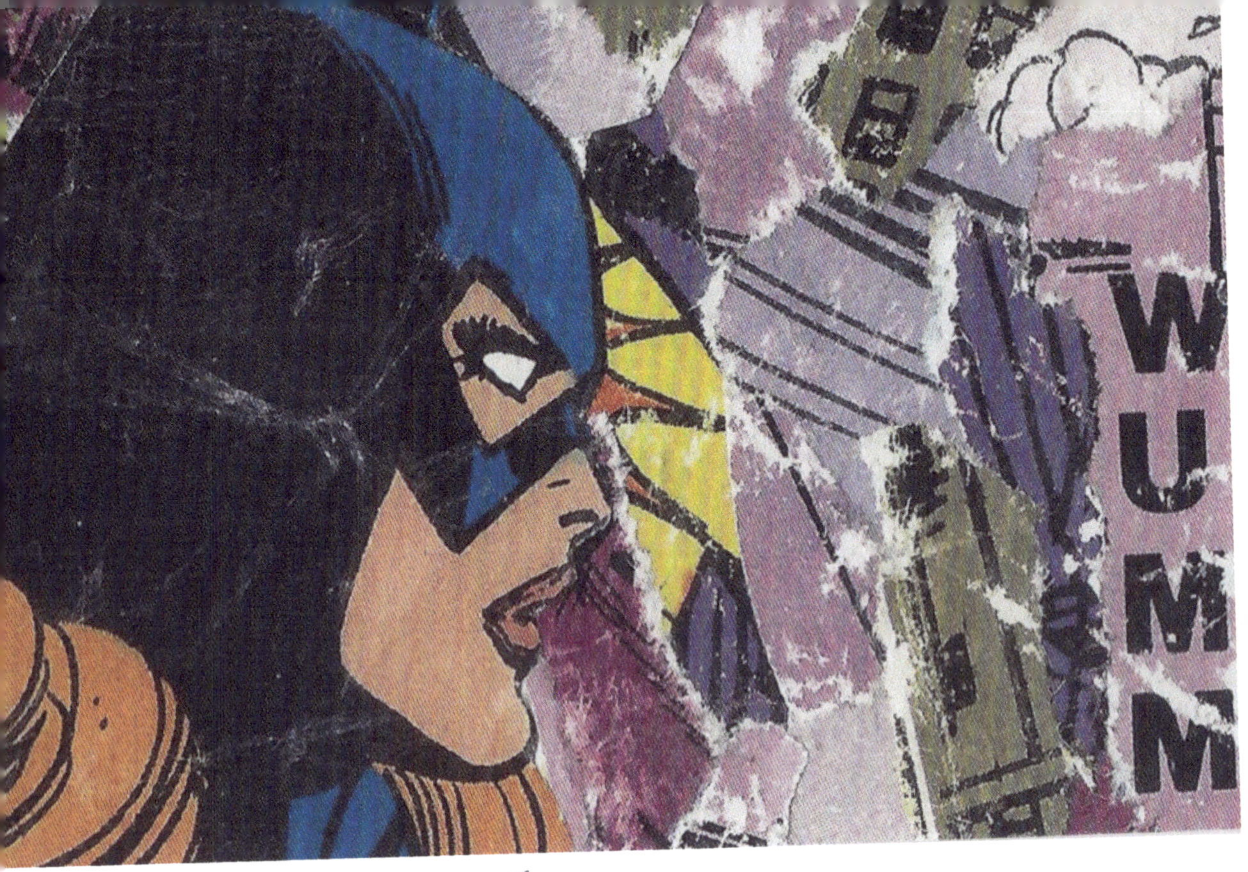

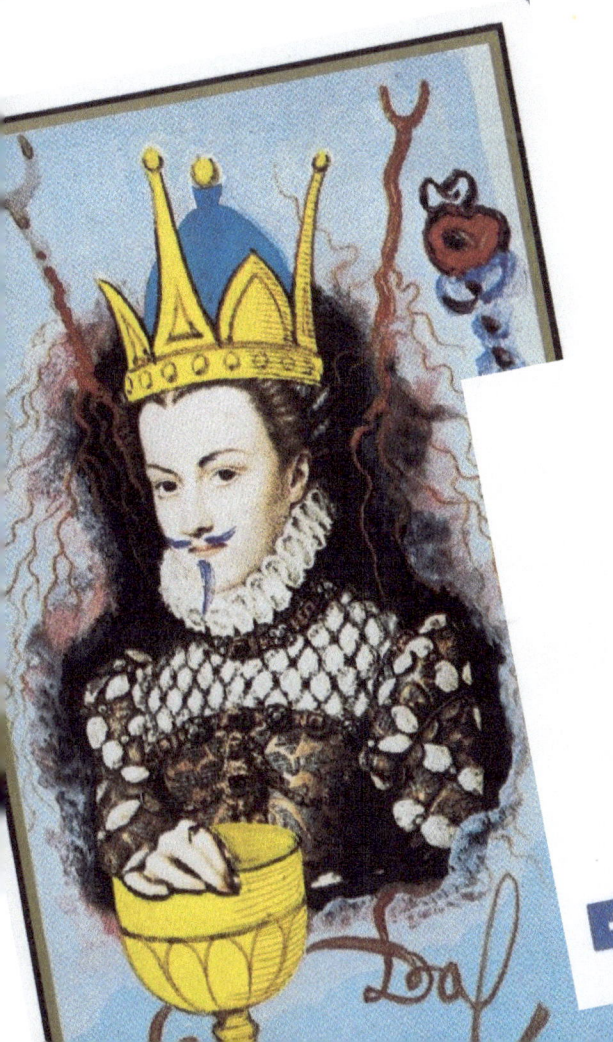

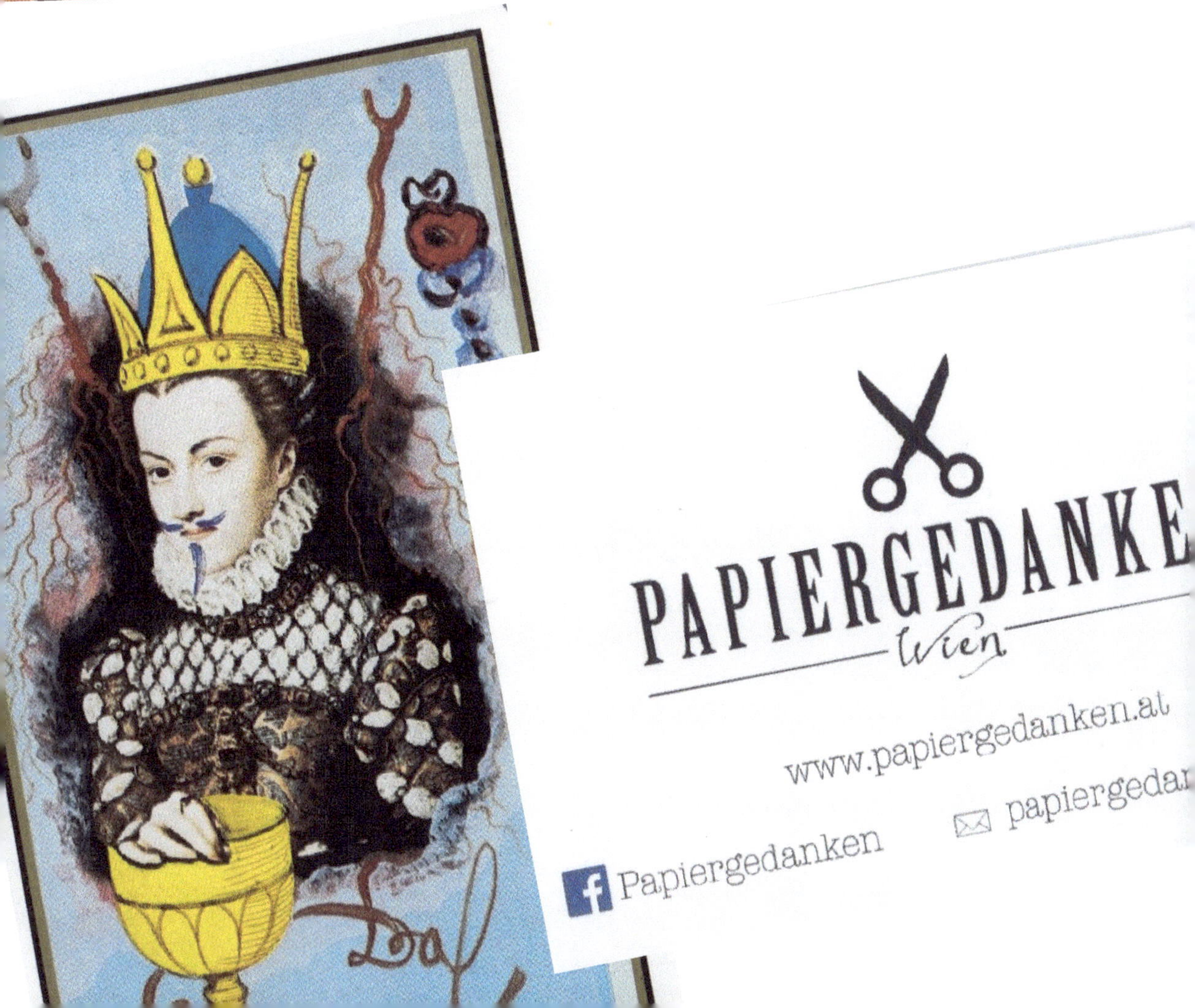

WUMM

PAPIERGEDANKE
Wien

www.papiergedanken.at

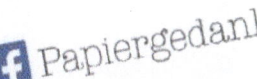 Papiergedanken   ✉ papiergedar

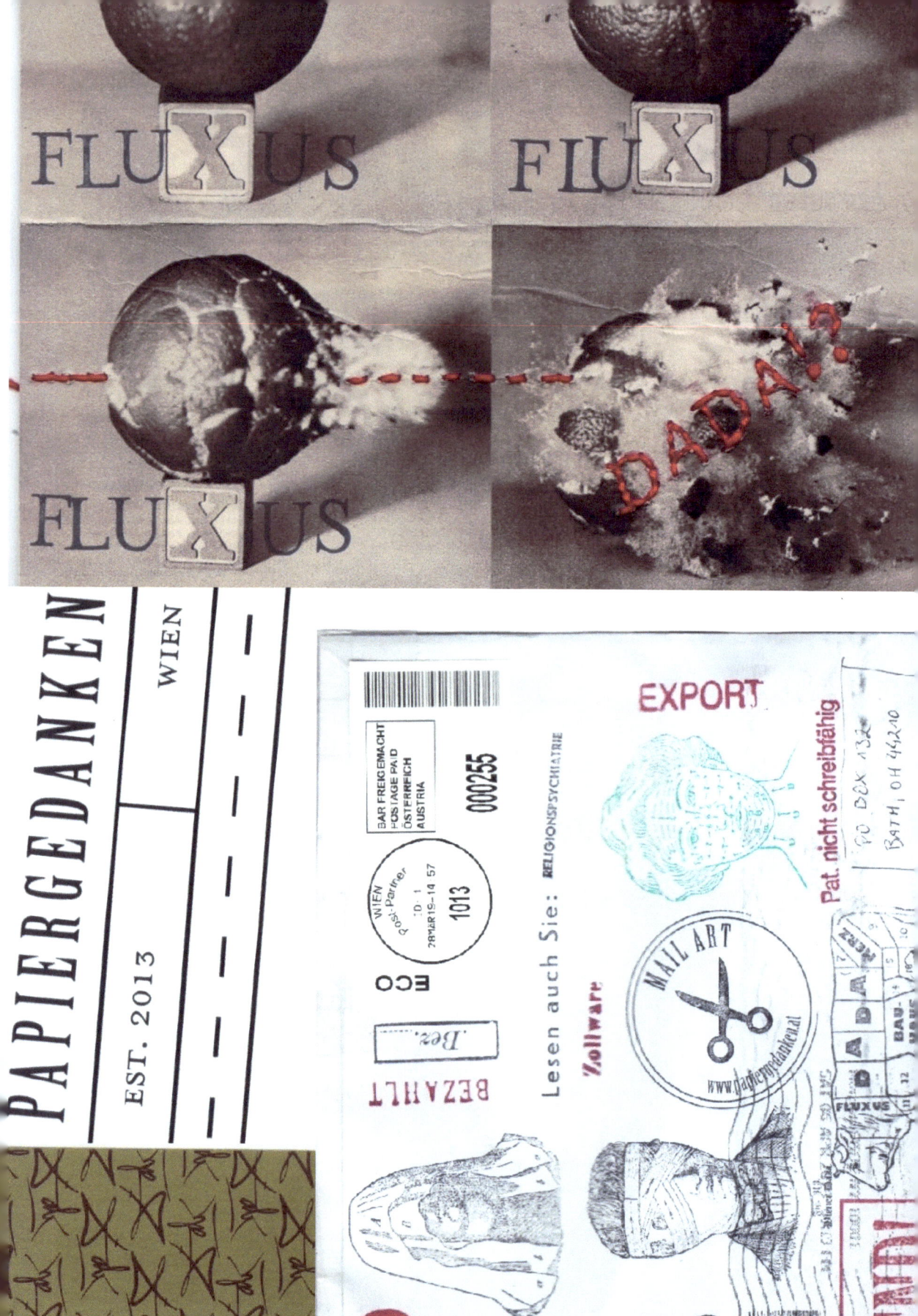

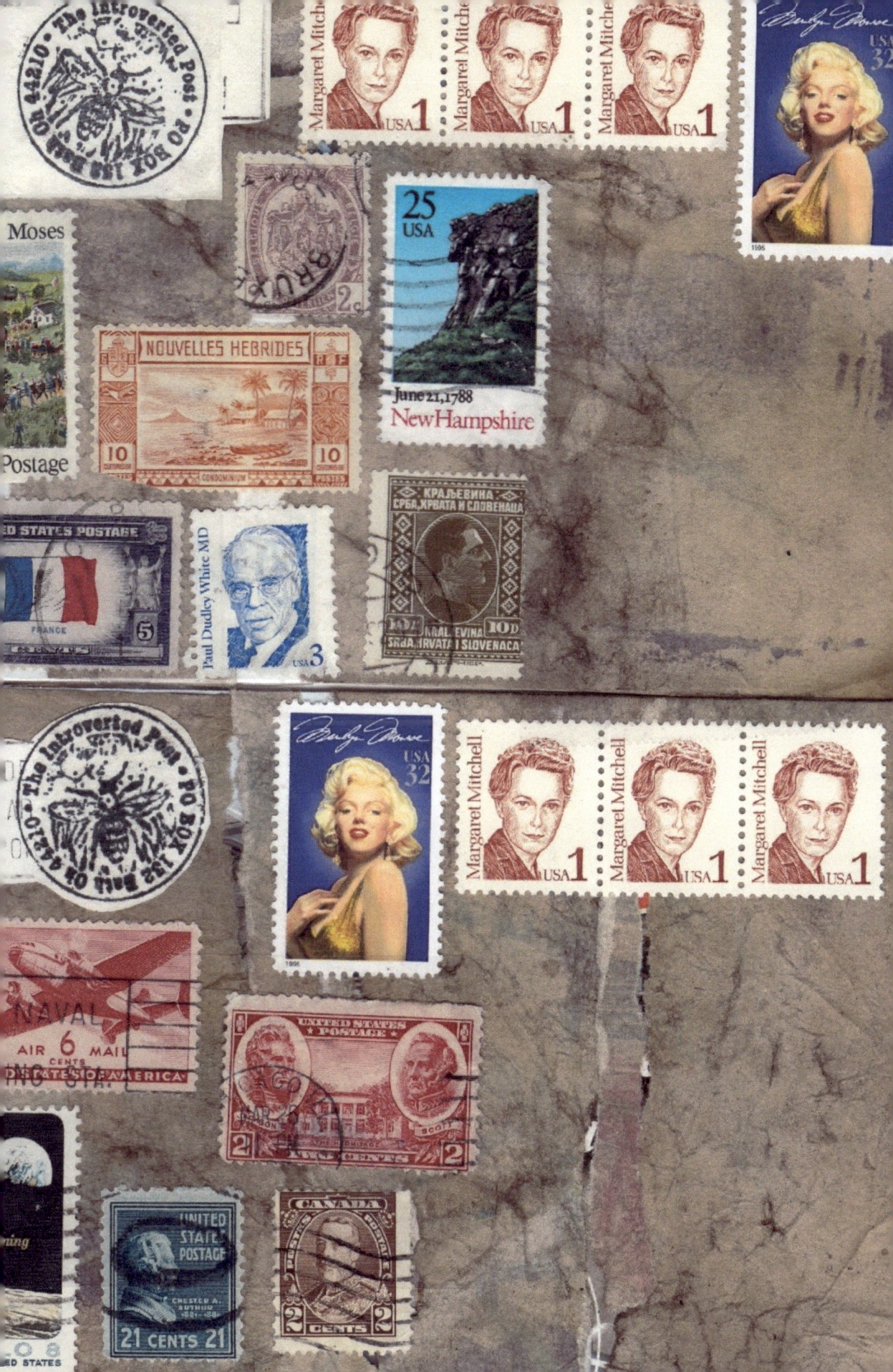

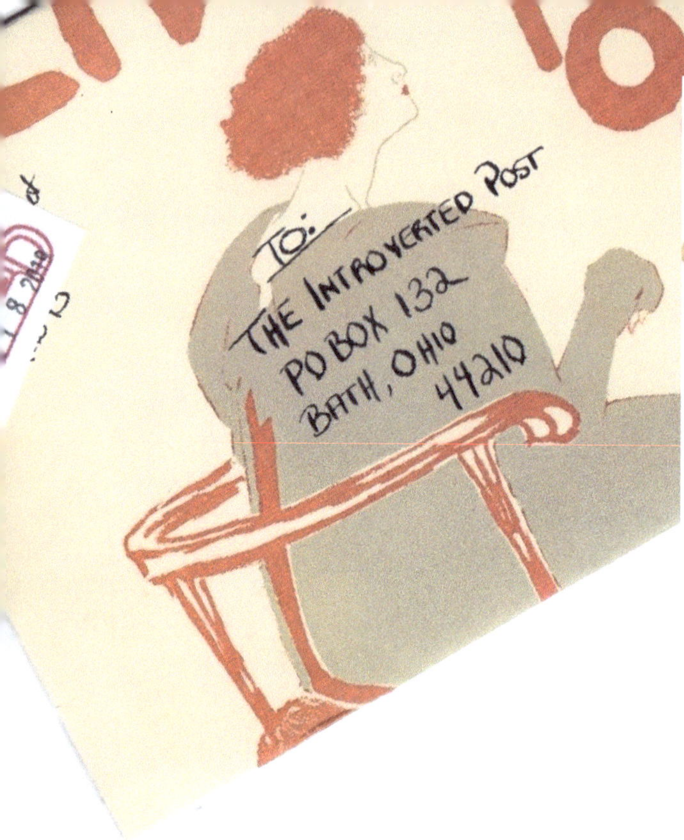

TO:
THE INTROVERTED POST
PO BOX 132
BATH, OHIO
44210

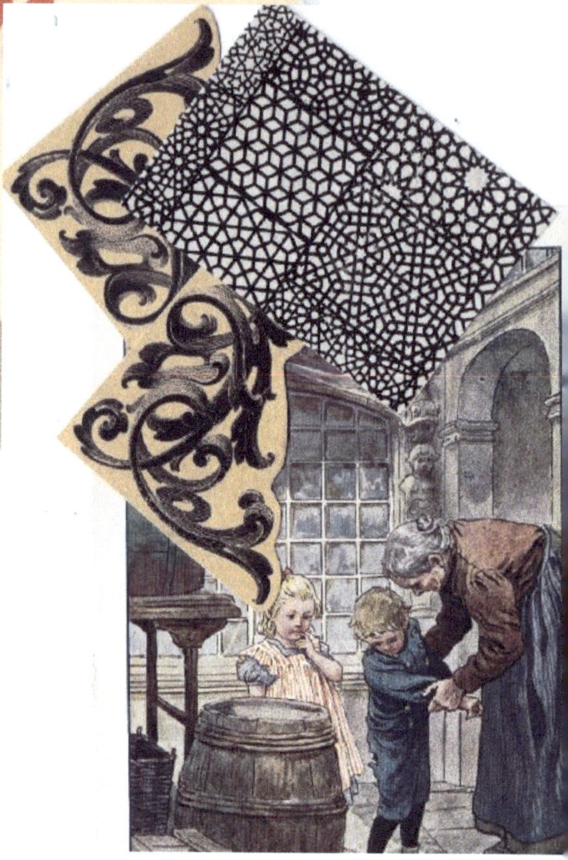

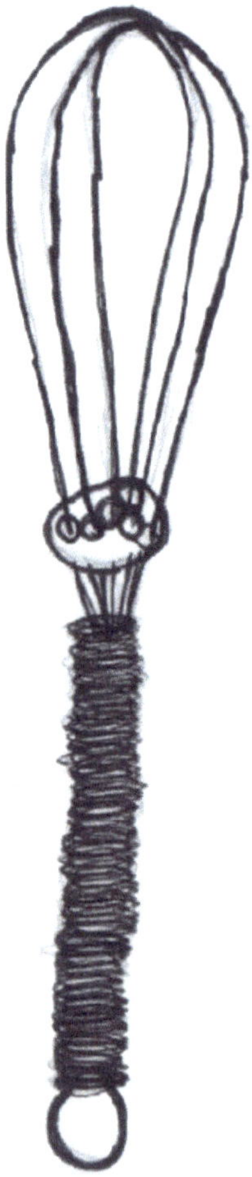

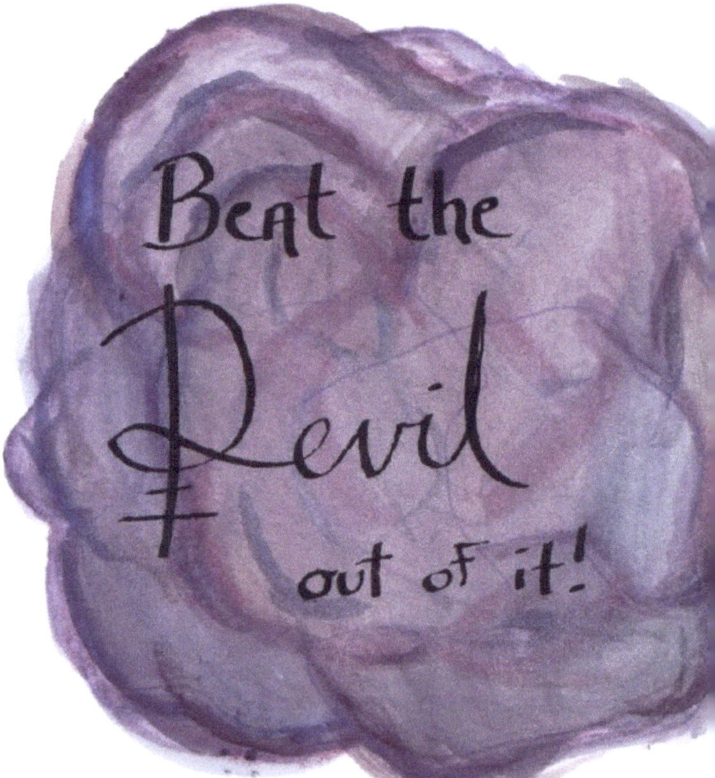

Beat the

Devil

out of it!

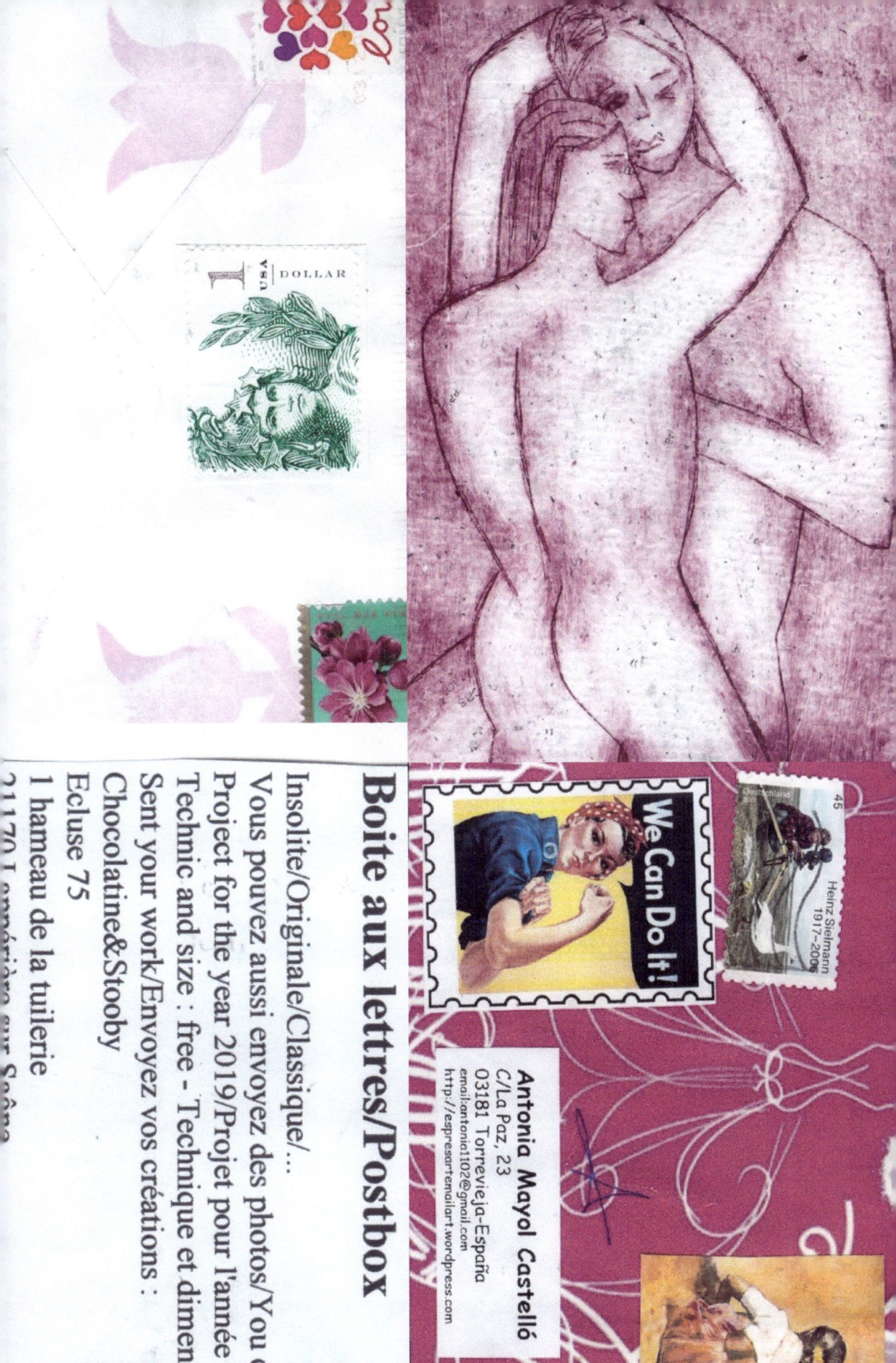

Antonia Mayol Castelló
C/La Paz, 23
03181 Torrevieja-España
emailantonia1102@gmail.com
http://espresartemailart.wordpress.com

Boite aux lettres/Postbox

Insolite/Originale/Classique/…
Vous pouvez aussi envoyez des photos/You c
Project for the year 2019/Projet pour l'année
Technic and size : free - Technique et dimens
Sent your work/Envoyez vos créations :
Chocolatine&Stooby
Ecluse 75
1 hameau de la tuilerie

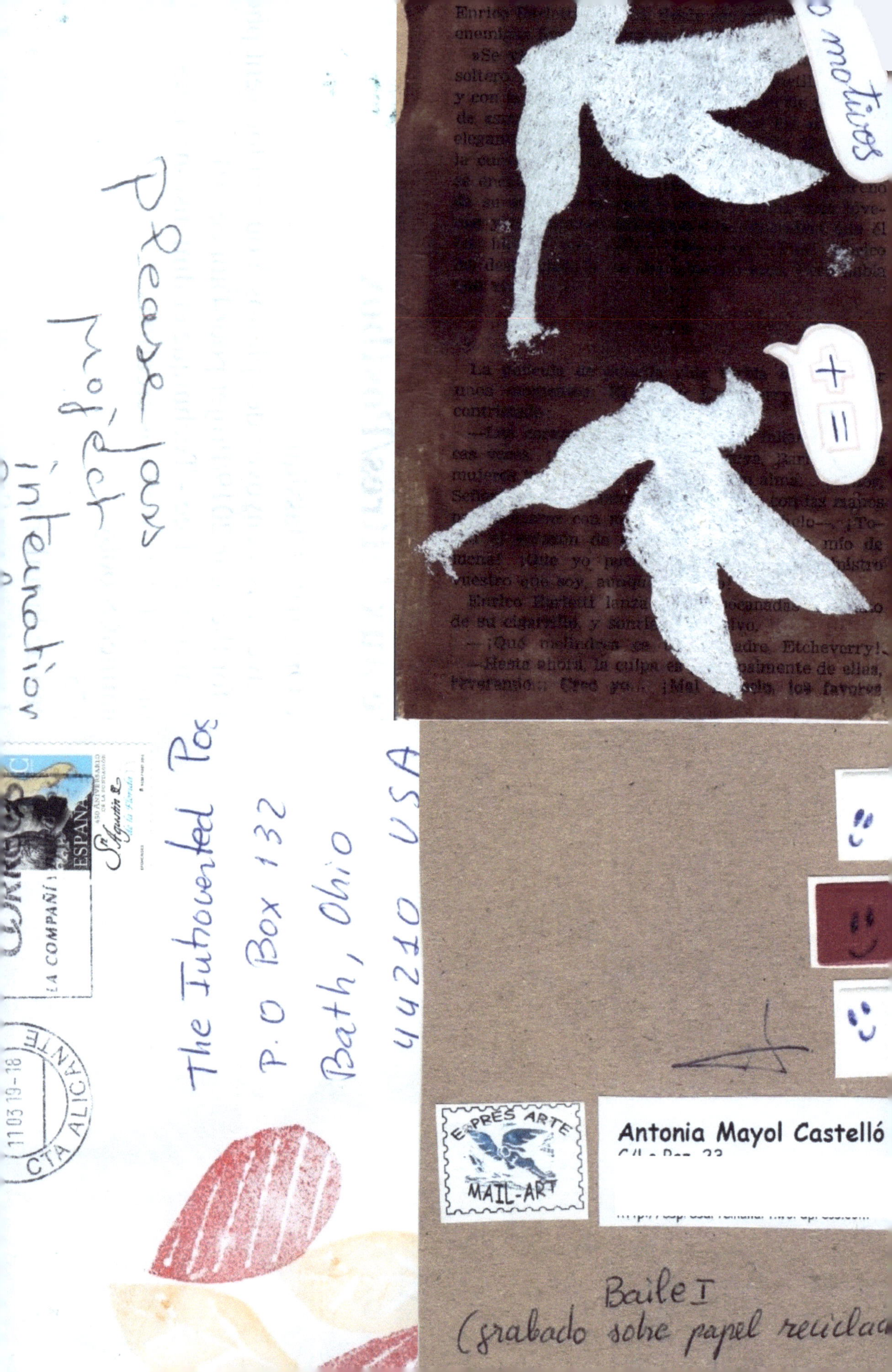

Please
Mojdch
internation

The Intouerted Pos
P.O Box 132
Bath, Ohio
44210 USA

ESPAÑA

CTA ALICANTE

EXPRÉS ARTE
MAIL-ART

Antonia Mayol Castelló

motivos

Baile I
(grabado sobre papel reciclad

Evans City Public

Mail Art Show

...w it at the library" or "Things

September –Novembe...

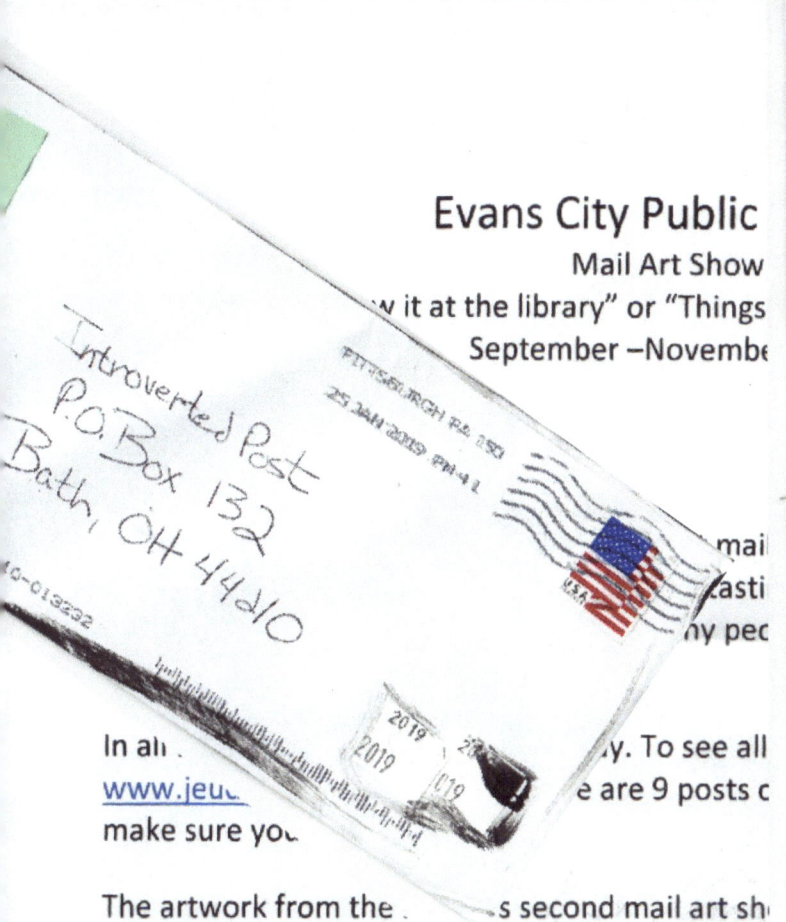

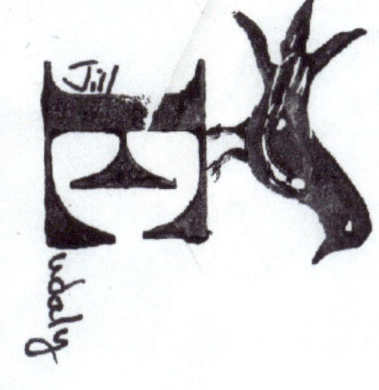

In al... ...y. To see all

www.jeud... ...e are 9 posts o...

make sure you...

The artwork from the ... ...s second mail art sh...
posted on the blog soon.
Plans are in the works for more mail art shows!

The Evans City Public Library staff and board members were overwhelmed by the
generosity of artist from around the world. Thank you for being part of our event.

Keep the snail mail coming!
Jill Eudaly
Evans City Public Library
205 S. Jackson St.
Evans City, PA 16033

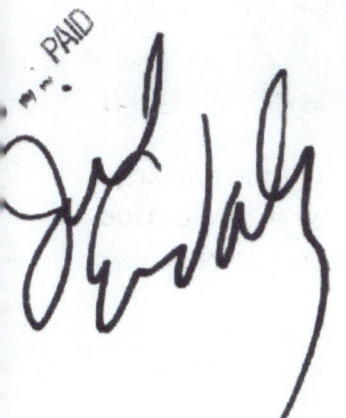

PAID

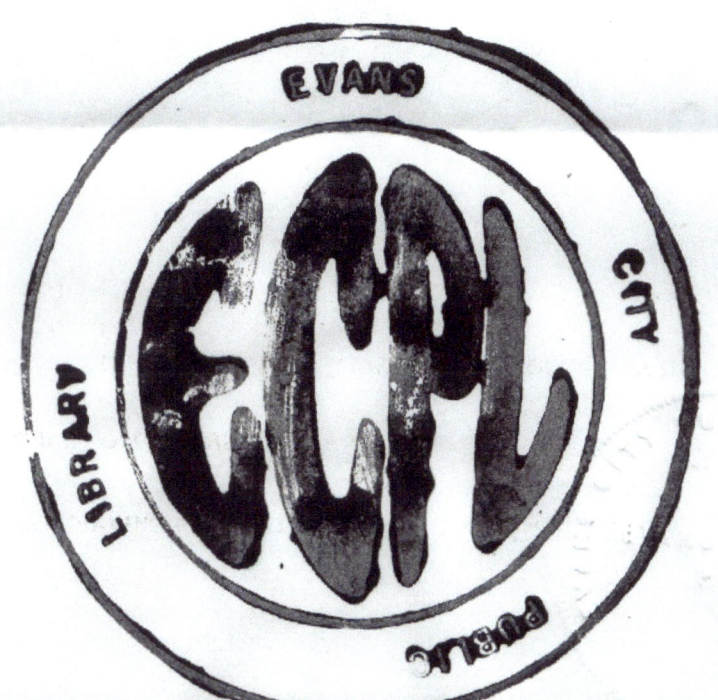

EVANS CITY PUBLIC LIBRARY
ECPL

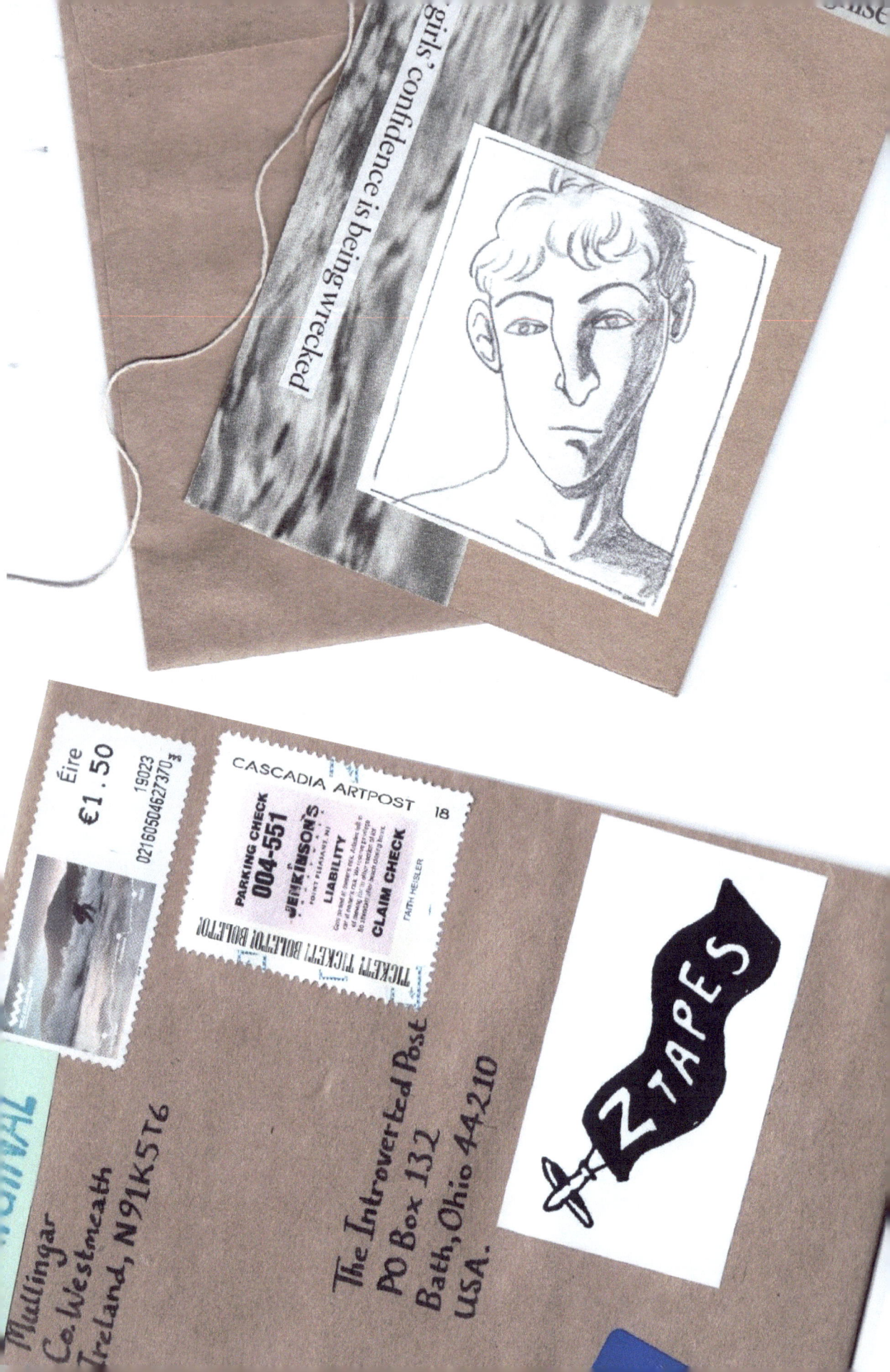

girl's confidence is being wrecked

Éire
€1.50
19023
0216050462737O₃₃

CASCADIA ARTPOST 18

PARKING CHECK
004-551
JENKINSON'S
POINT PLEASANT, NJ
LIABILITY
CLAIM CHECK
FAITH HEISLER

TICKETT BOLLETTOI BOLLETTOI TICKETT

Z TAPES

The Introverted Post
PO Box 132
Bath, Ohio 44210
USA.

Mullingar
Co. Westmeath
Ireland, N91K5T6

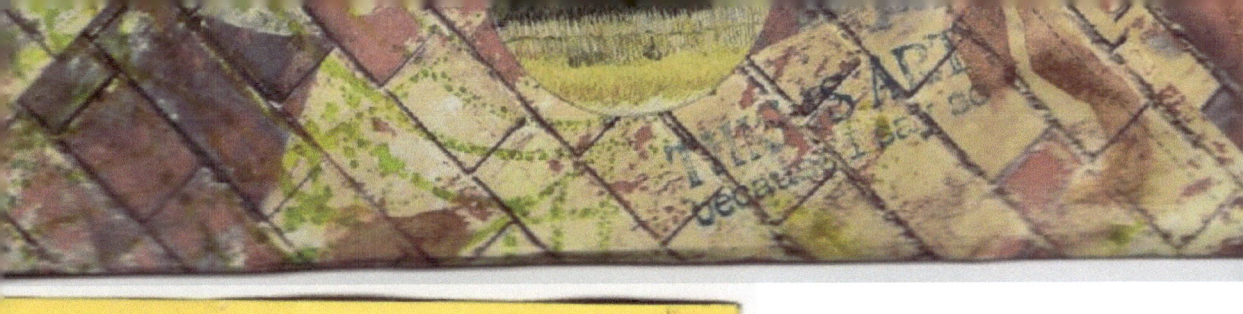

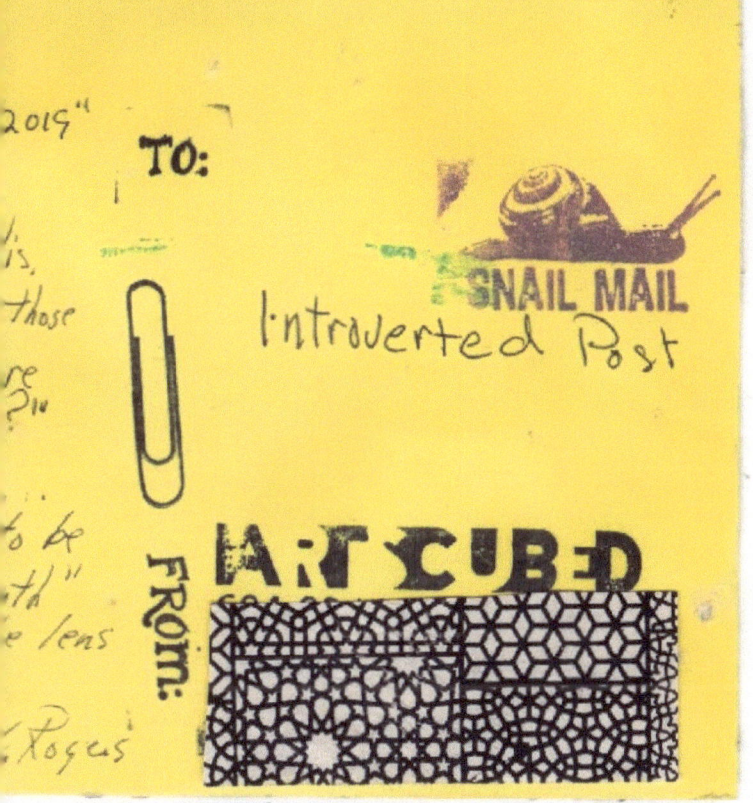

2019"

TO:

i5,

those

re

?"

to be

d"

e lens

Rogus

SNAIL MAIL

Introverted Post

FROM:

ArT CUBeD

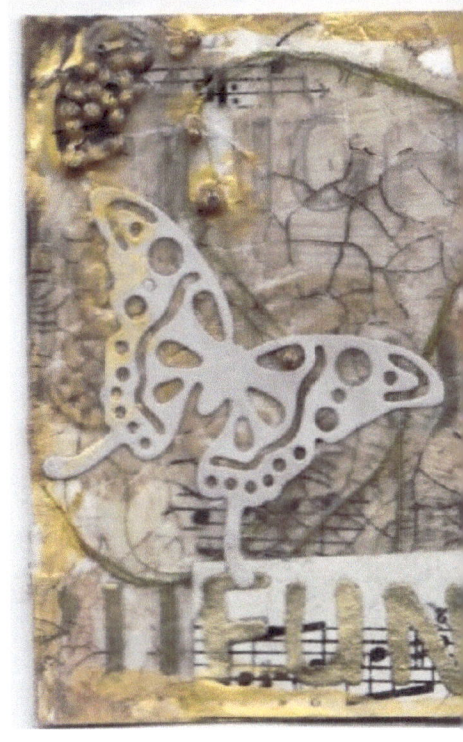

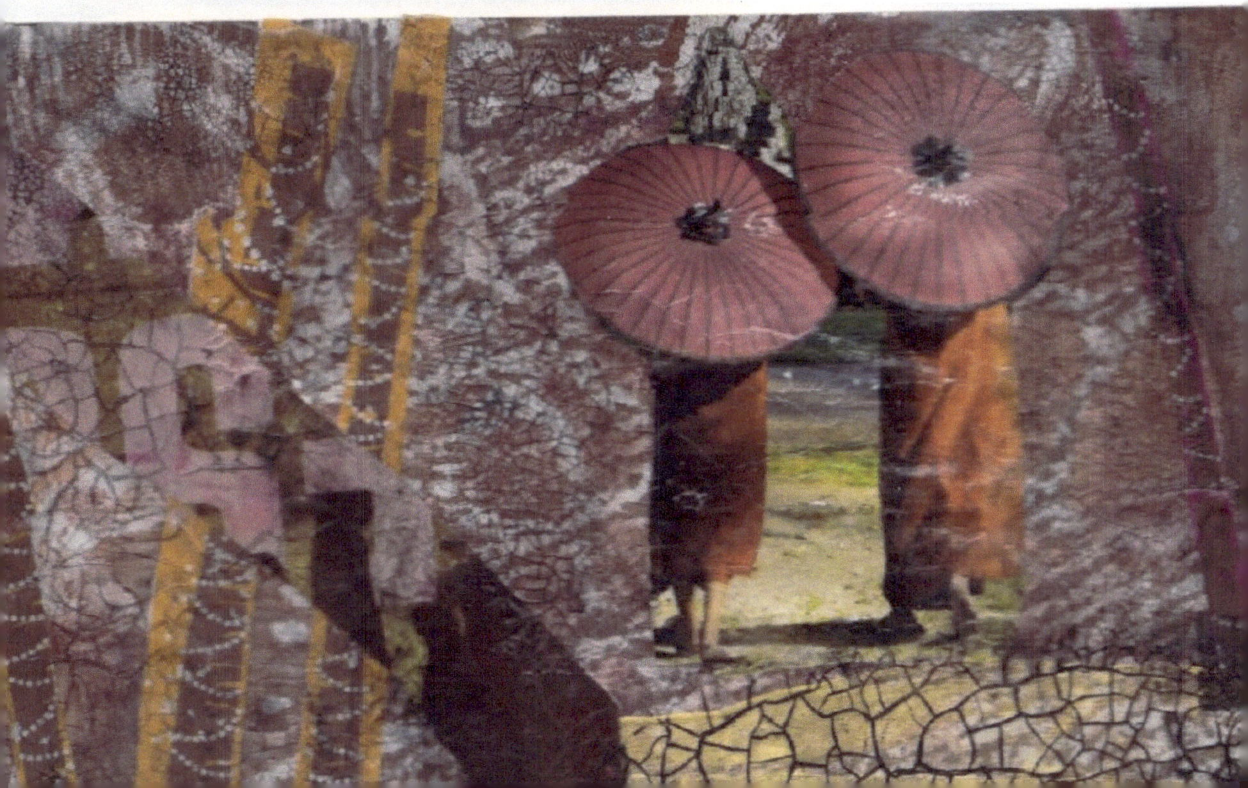

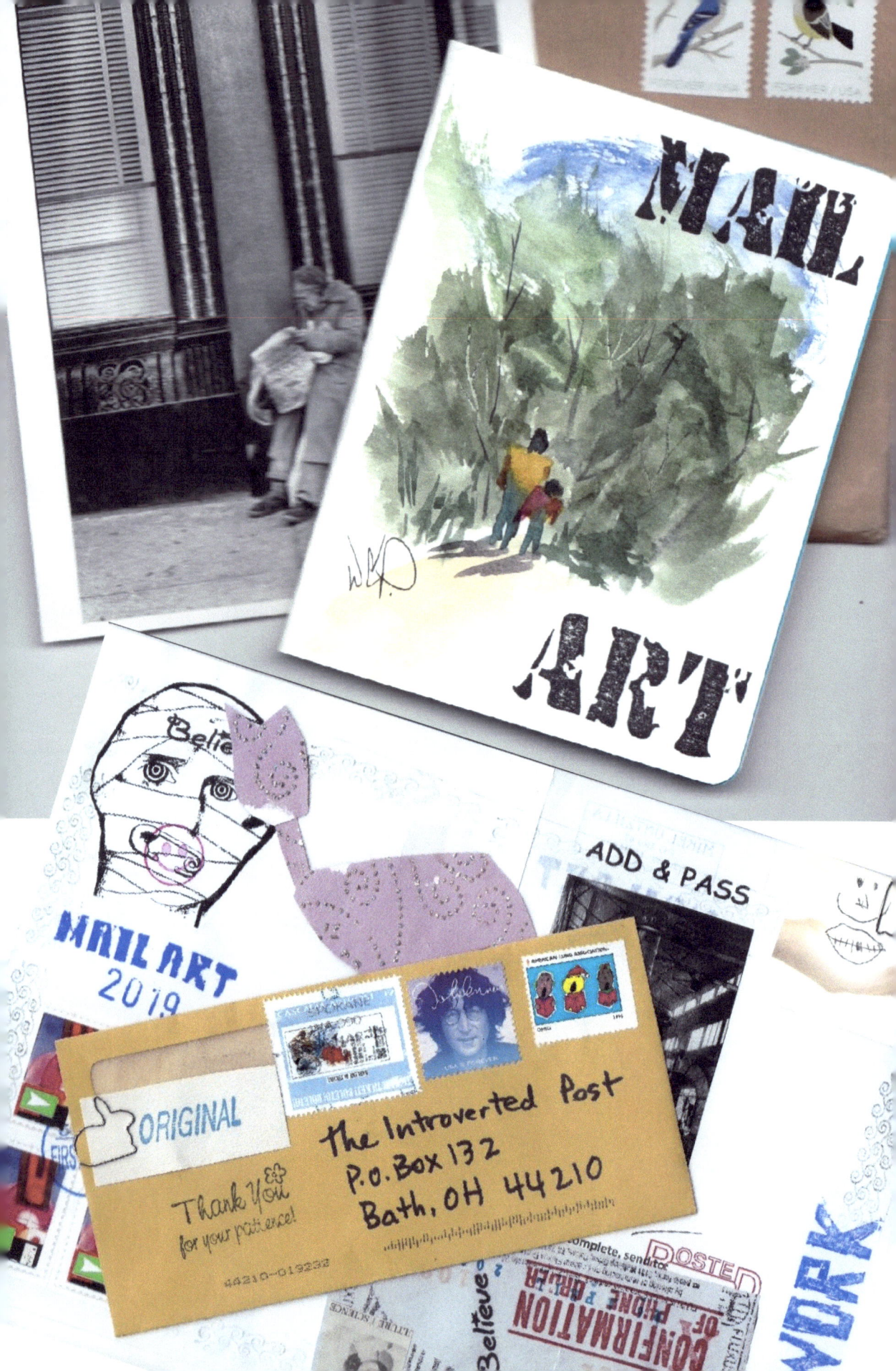

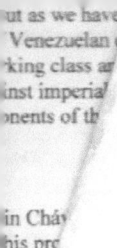

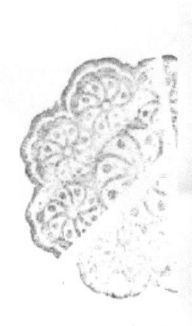

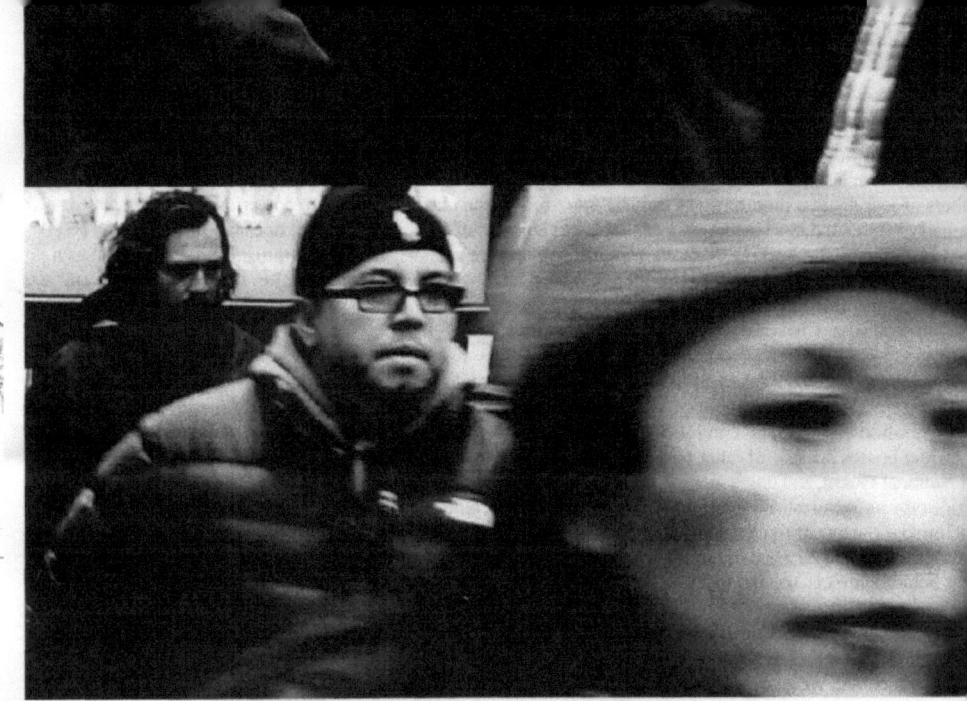

ut as we have
Venezuelan
king class a
inst imperial
onents of th

in Chá
his pro
mme
So w
fare
re

ember what the dormouse said
d your head, feed your head

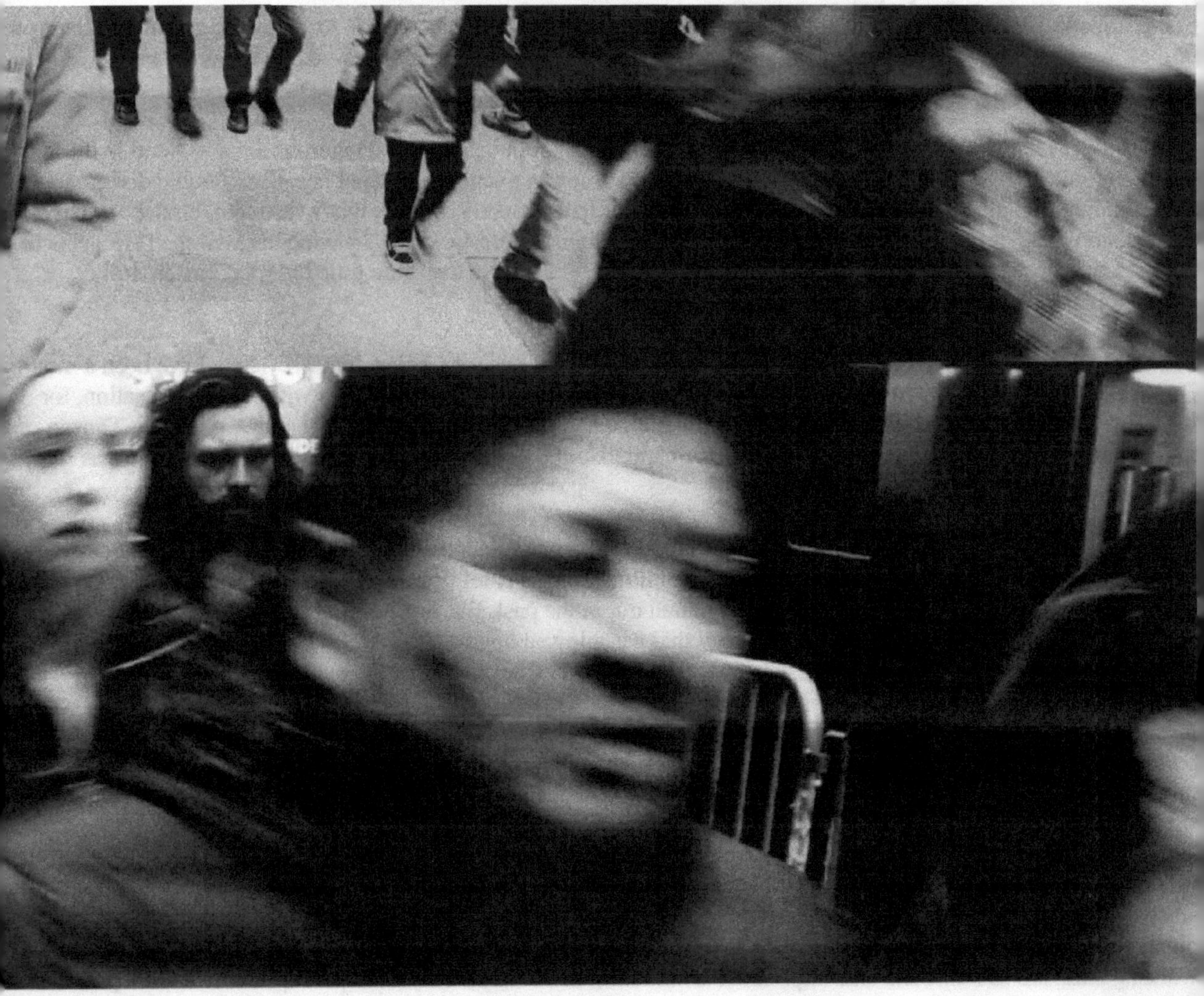

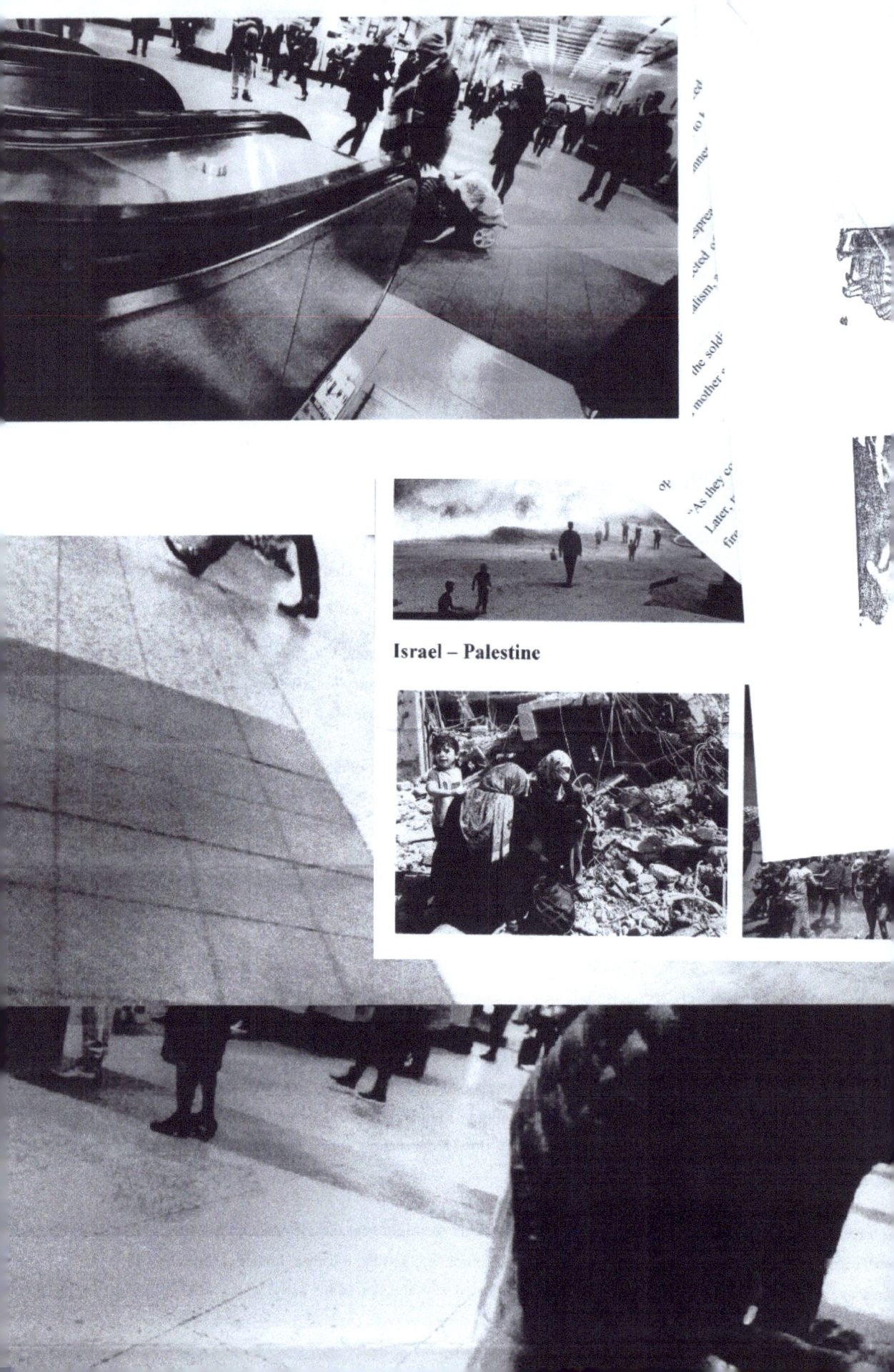

Israel – Palestine

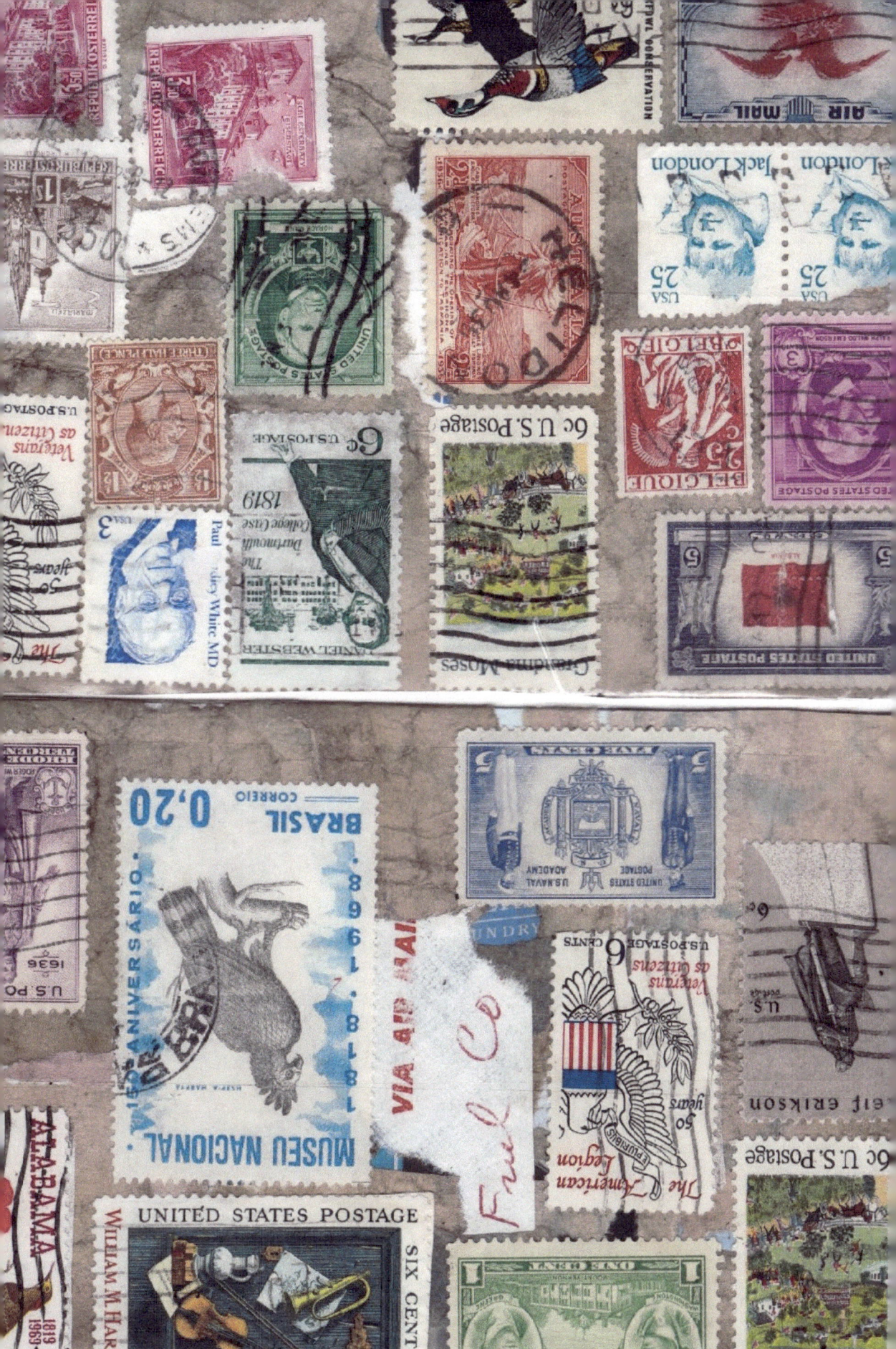

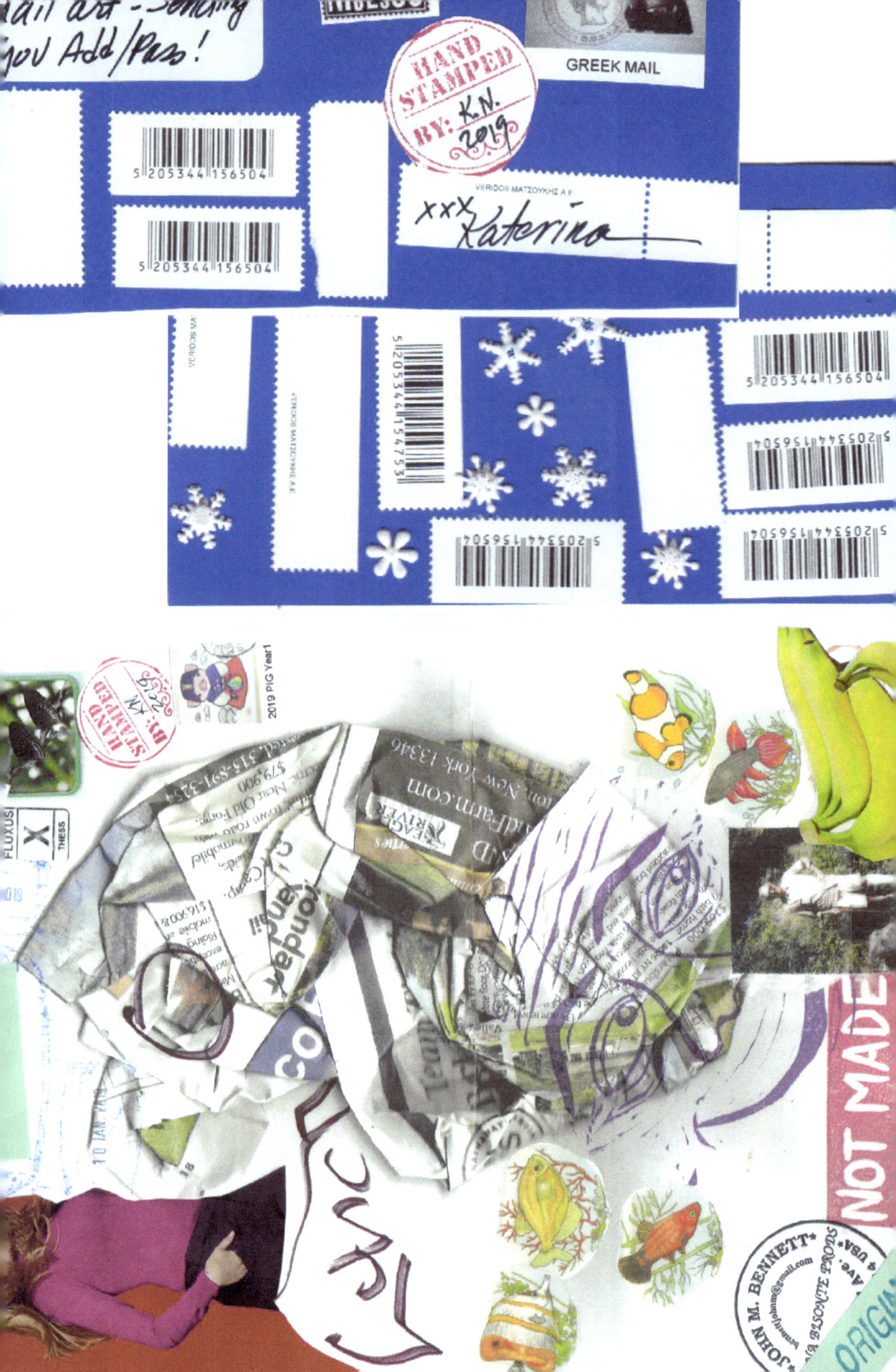

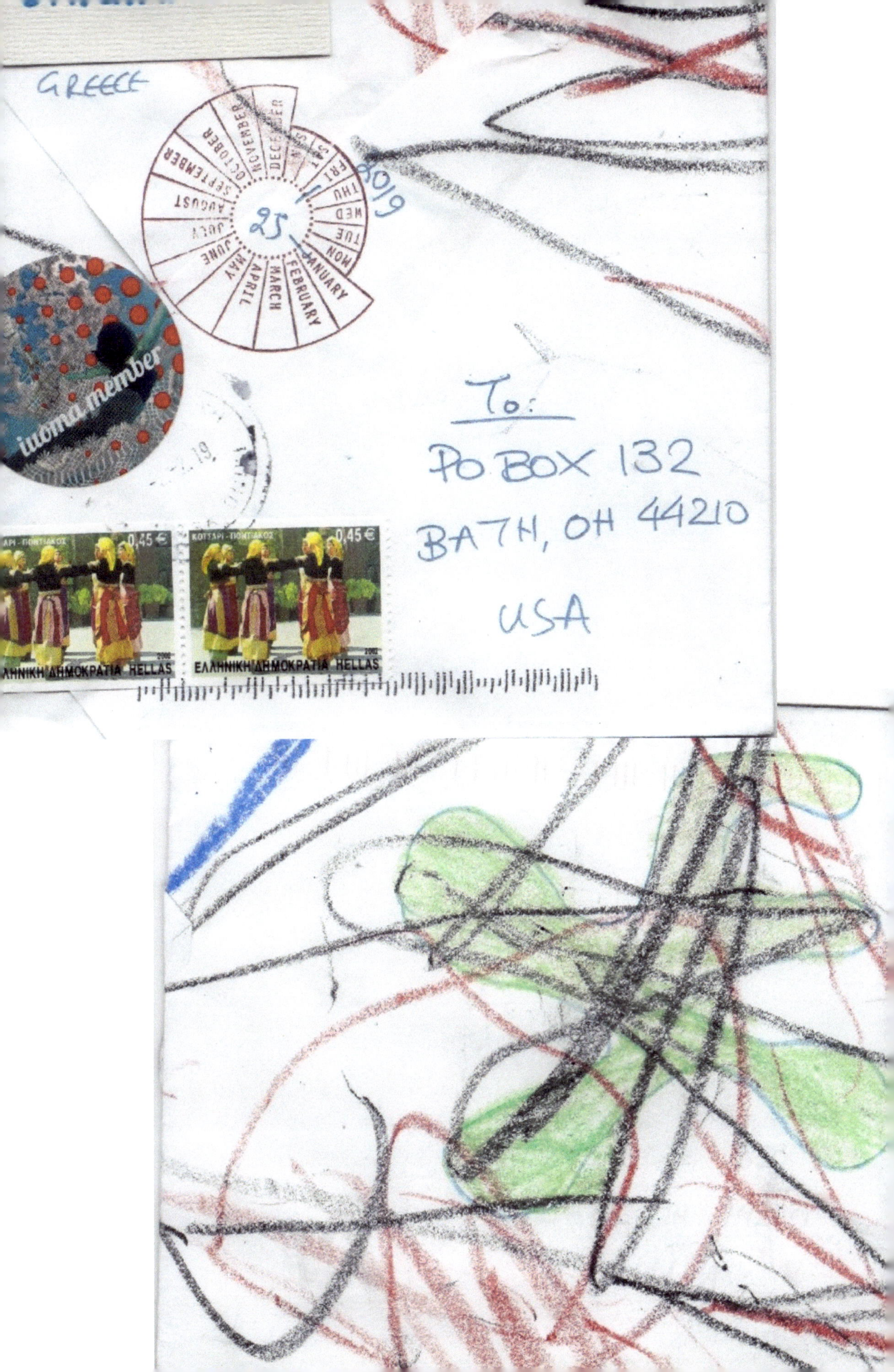

GREECE

25

2019

iwma member

ΑΡΙ - ΠΟΝΤΙΑΚΟΣ 0,45 €   ΚΟΤΣΑΡΙ - ΠΟΝΤΙΑΚΟΣ 0,45 €

ΕΛΛΗΝΙΚΗ ΔΗΜΟΚΡΑΤΙΑ HELLAS   ΕΛΛΗΝΙΚΗ ΔΗΜΟΚΡΑΤΙΑ HELLAS

To:
P.O BOX 132
BATH, OH 44210

USA

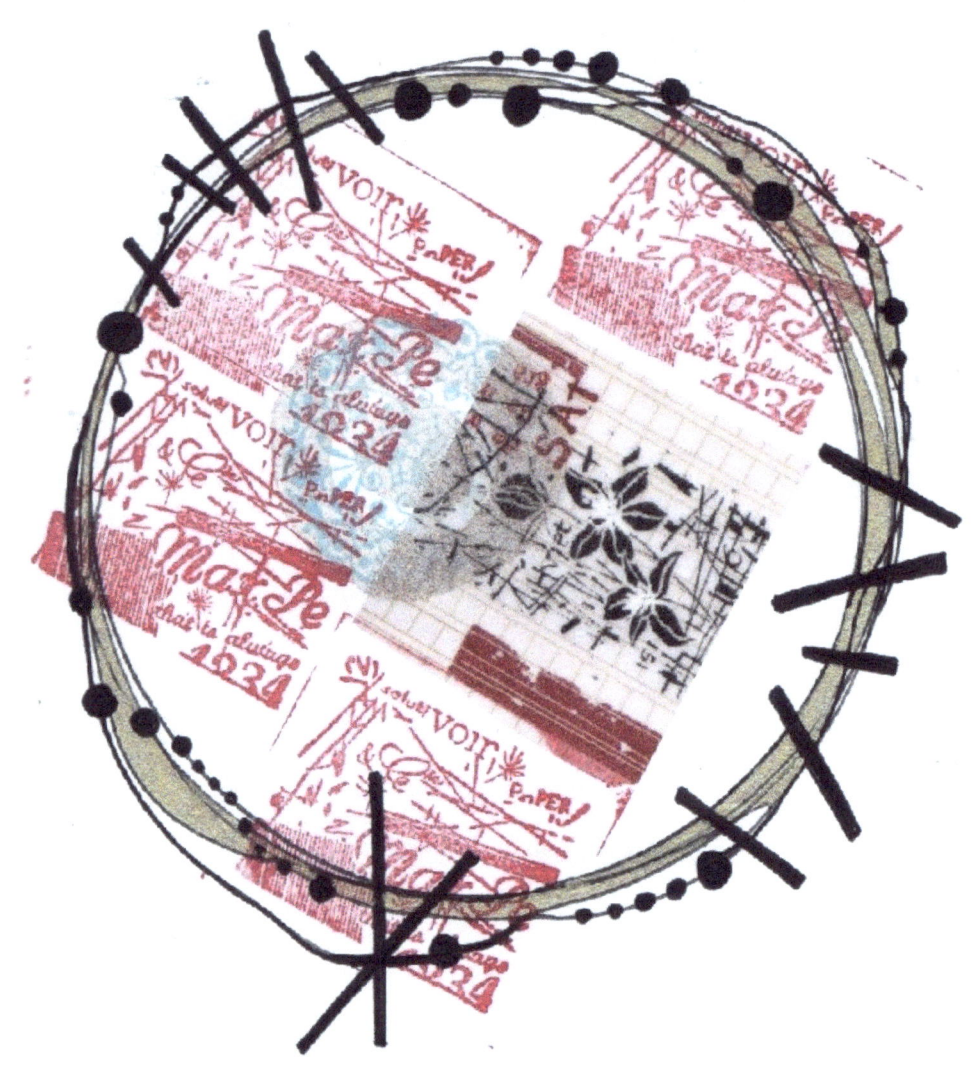

Georgia Grigoriadou 20

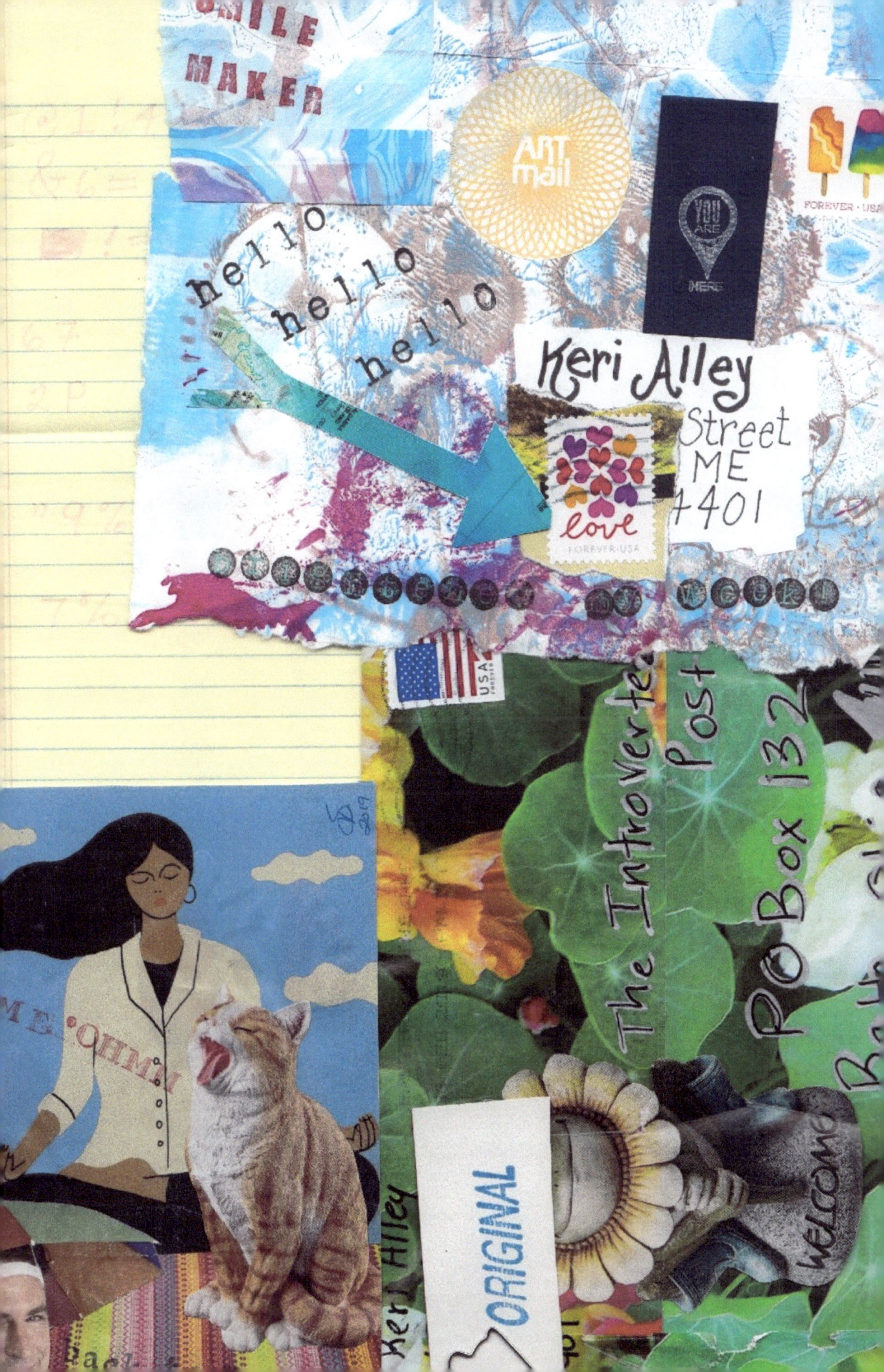

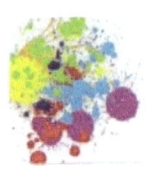

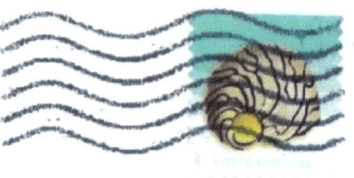

The Introve...
PO Box 13...
Bath, OH ...

4210-013232

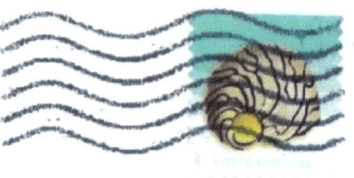

The Introverted Post
Quarterly Book of Mail Art
theintrovertedpost.com
@theintrovertedpost
PO Box 132
Bath, Ohio
44210
USA

The Introverted Post
Quarterly Book of Mail Art
theintrovertedpost.com
@theintrovertedpost
PO Box 132
Bath, Ohio
44210
USA

The Introverted Post
Quarterly Book of Mail Art
theintrovertedpost.com
@theintrovertedpost
PO Box 132
Bath, Ohio
44210
USA

The Introverted Post
Quarterly Book of Mail Art
theintrovertedpost.com
@theintrovertedpost
PO Box 132
Bath, Ohio
44210
USA

The Introverted Post
Quarterly Book of Mail Art
theintrovertedpost.com
@theintrovertedpost
PO Box 132
Bath, Ohio
44210
USA

The Introverted Post

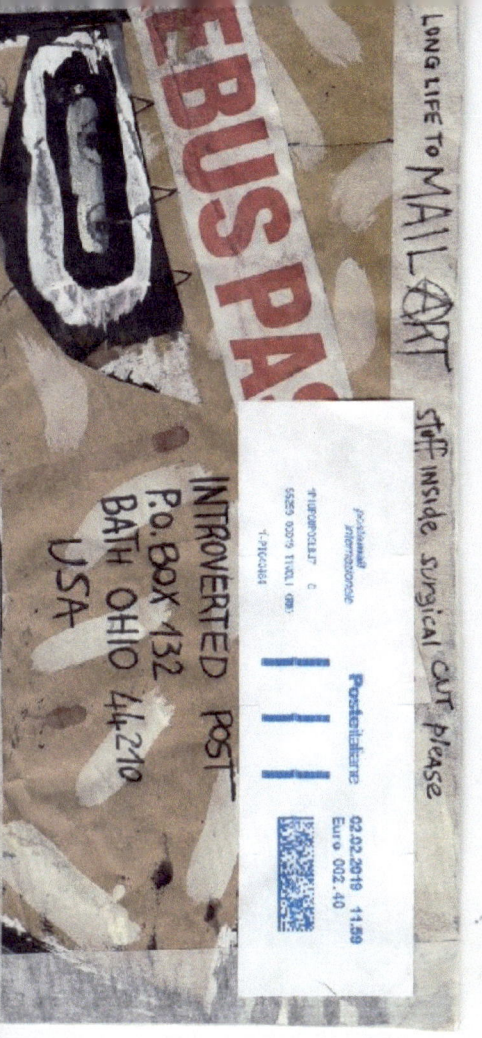

LONG LIFE TO MAIL ART

Stuff inside surgical cut please

INTROVERTED POST
P.O.Box 132
BATH OHIO 44210
USA

REBUS PA

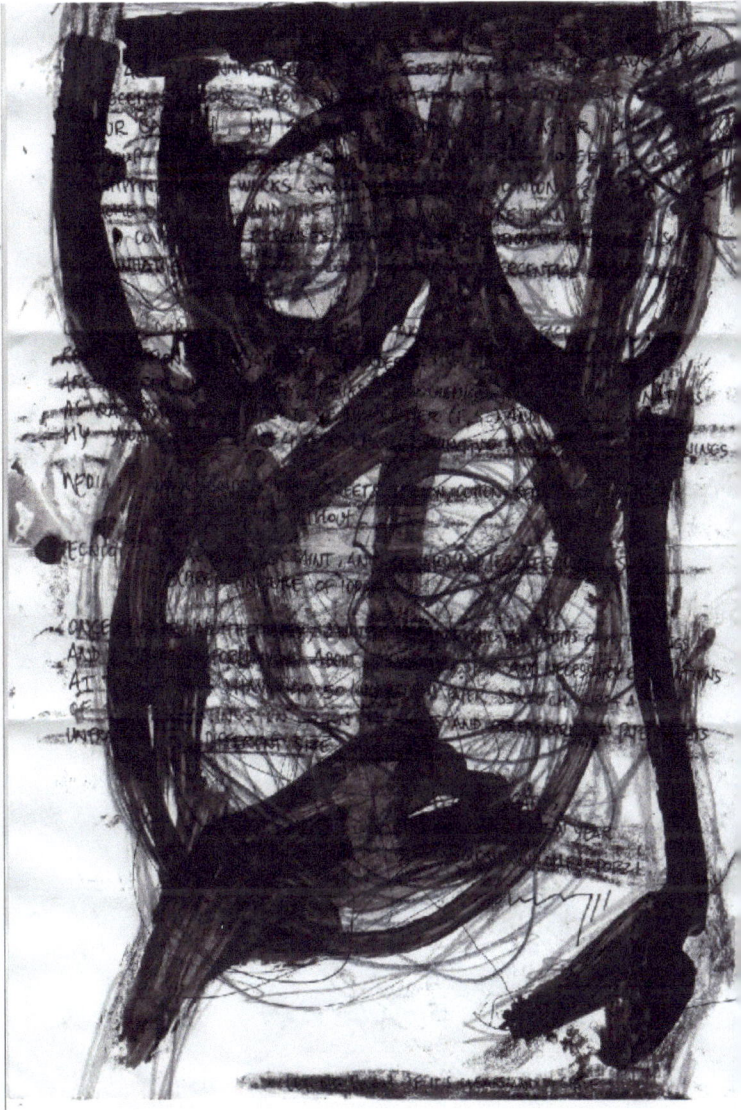

IPOTESI DIARREA

MITT: GIOVANNI LOMBARDOZZI

PENNY FOR YOUR

GULFPORT
33707

Anchor Envelopes

The Introverted Post
PO BOX 132
Bath, Ohio 44210

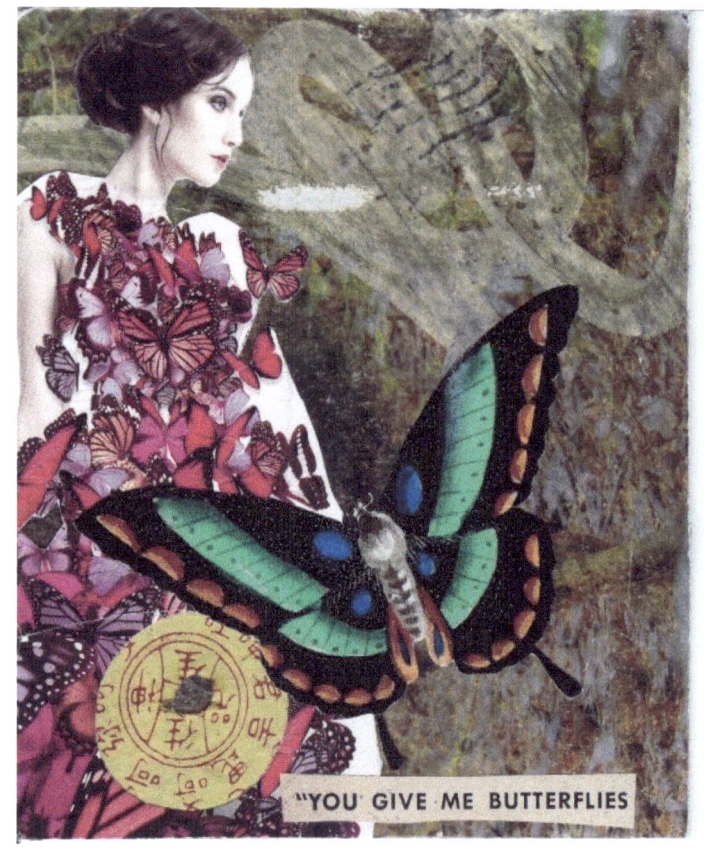

"YOU GIVE ME BUTTERFLIES

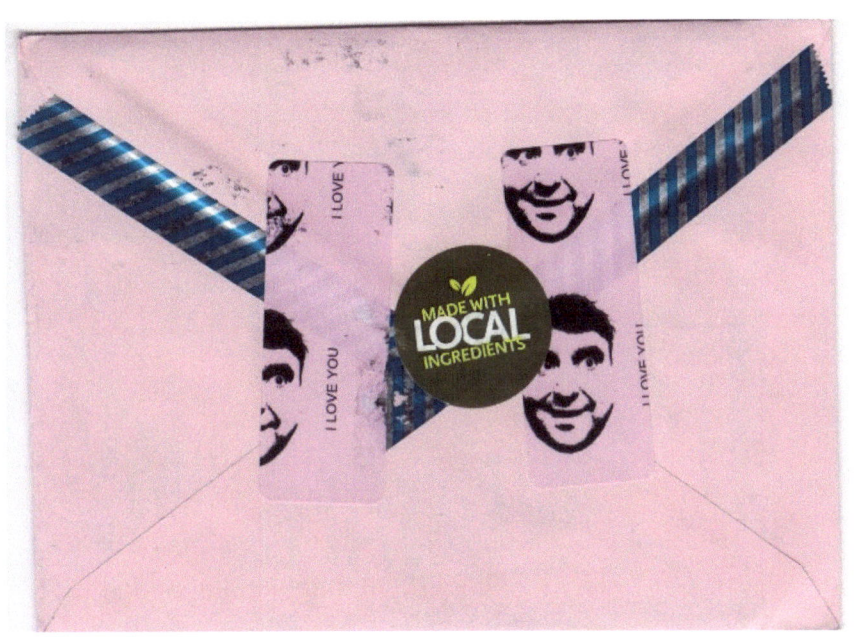

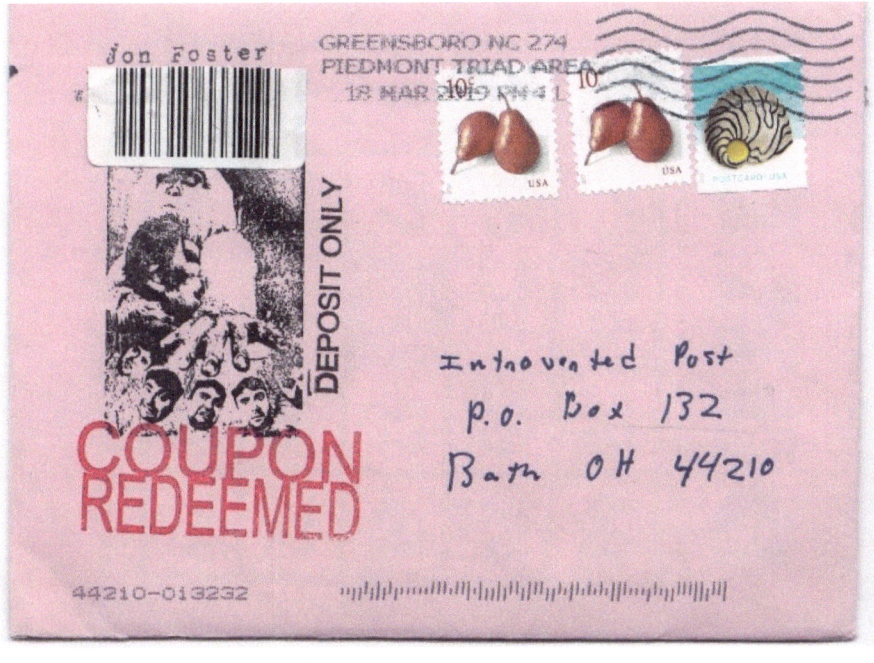

Jon Foster

GREENSBORO NC 274
PIEDMONT TRIAD AREA
18 MAR 2019 PM 4 L

DEPOSIT ONLY

COUPON
REDEEMED

44210-013232

Introverted Post
P.O. Box 132
Bath OH 44210

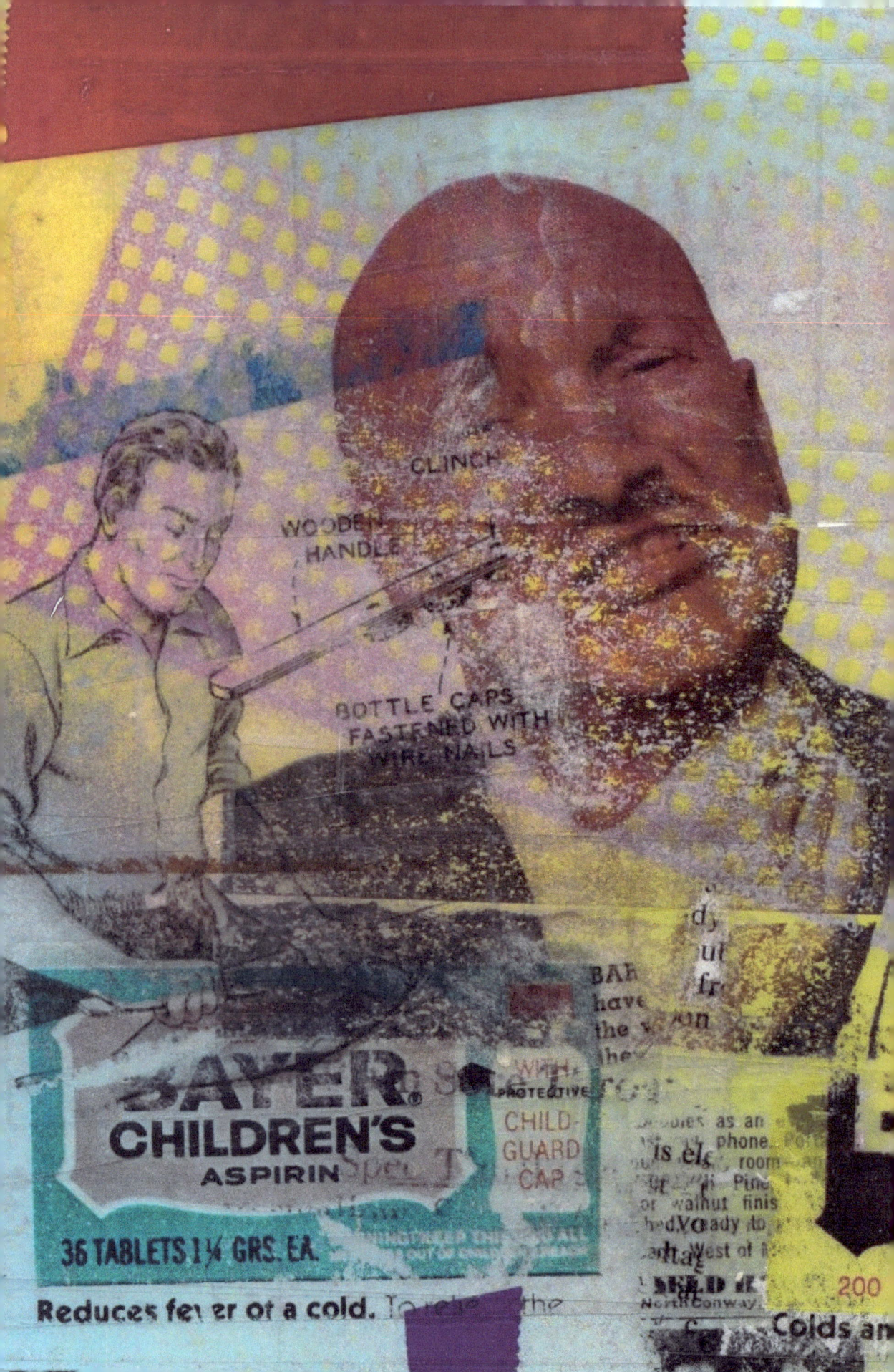

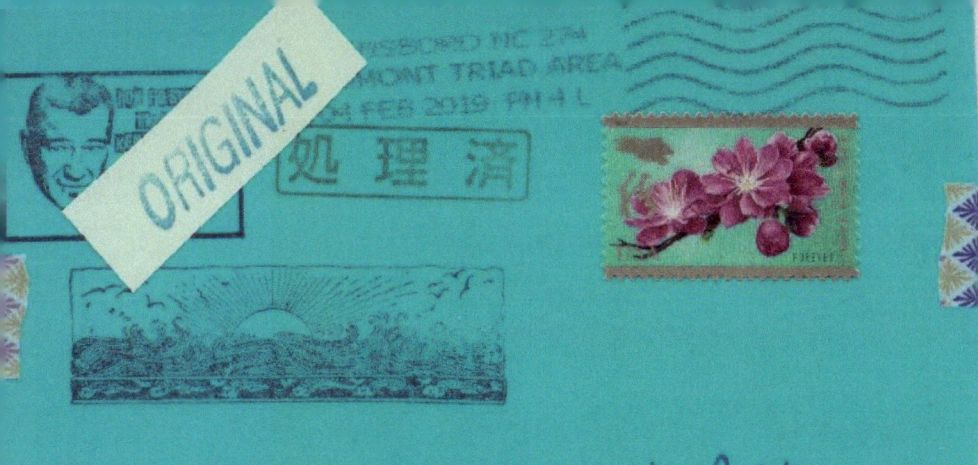

処理済

Introverted Post
P.o. Box 132
Bath Ohio 44210

44210-013232

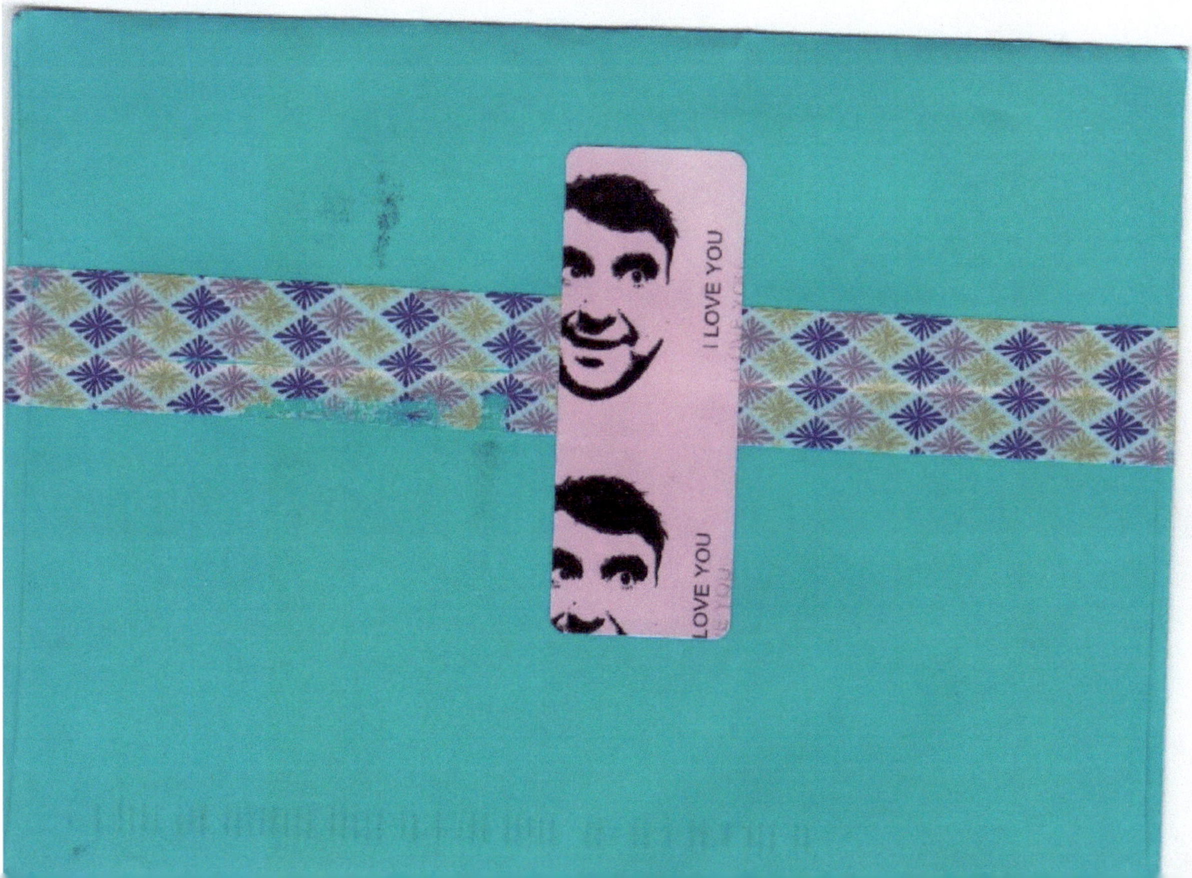

I LOVE YOU

I LOVE YOU

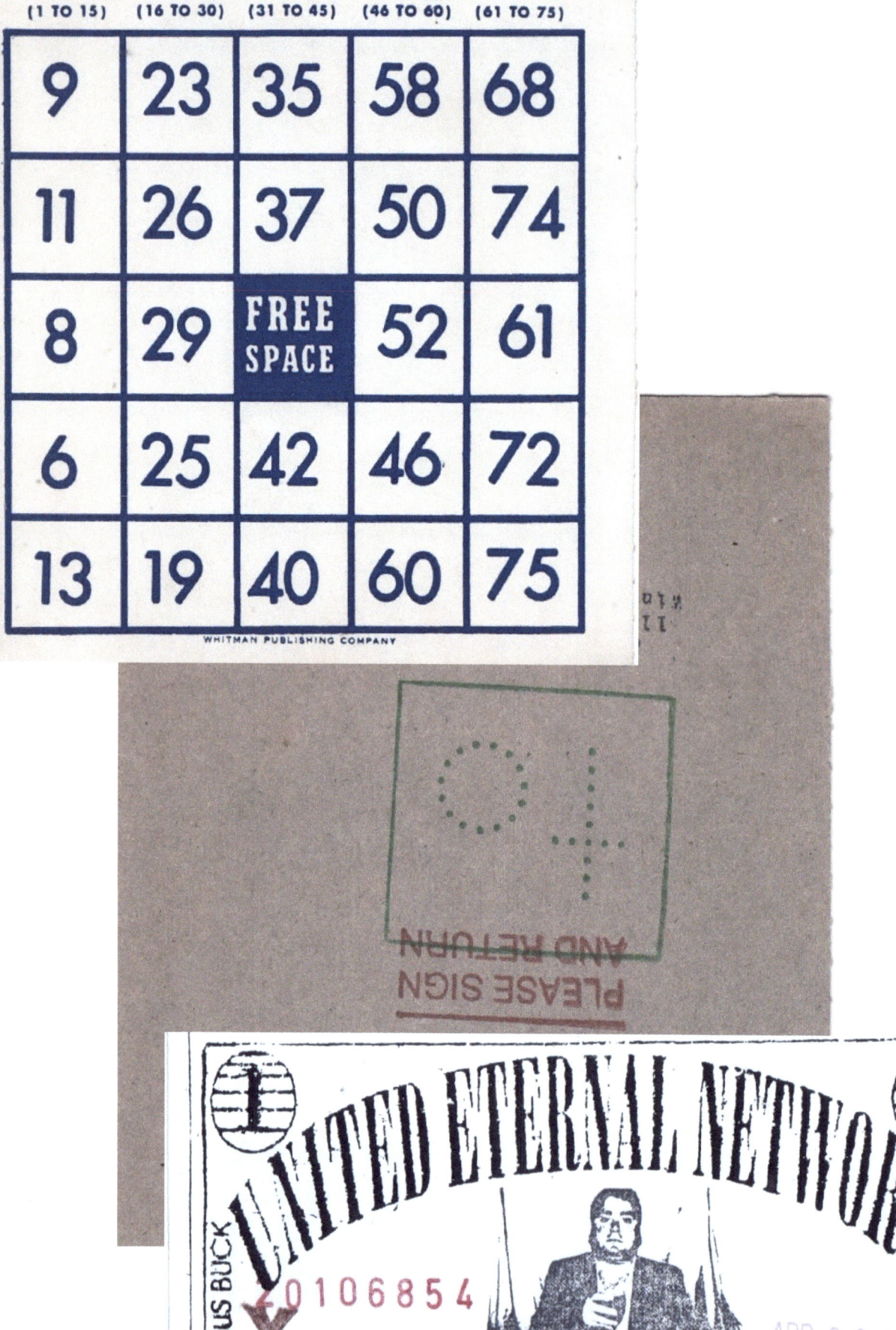

(1 TO 15)	(16 TO 30)	(31 TO 45)	(46 TO 60)	(61 TO 75)
9	23	35	58	68
11	26	37	50	74
8	29	FREE SPACE	52	61
6	25	42	46	72
13	19	40	60	75

WHITMAN PUBLISHING COMPANY

PLEASE SIGN AND RETURN

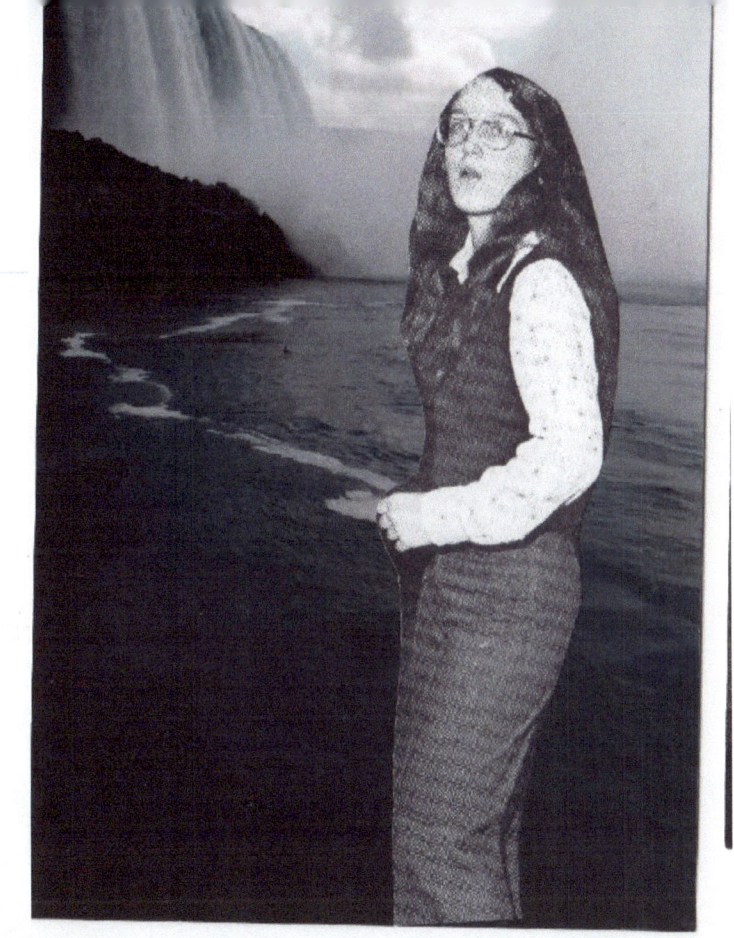

NIAGARA FALLS
        AUGUST 2017

    BY: MELISSA WAND

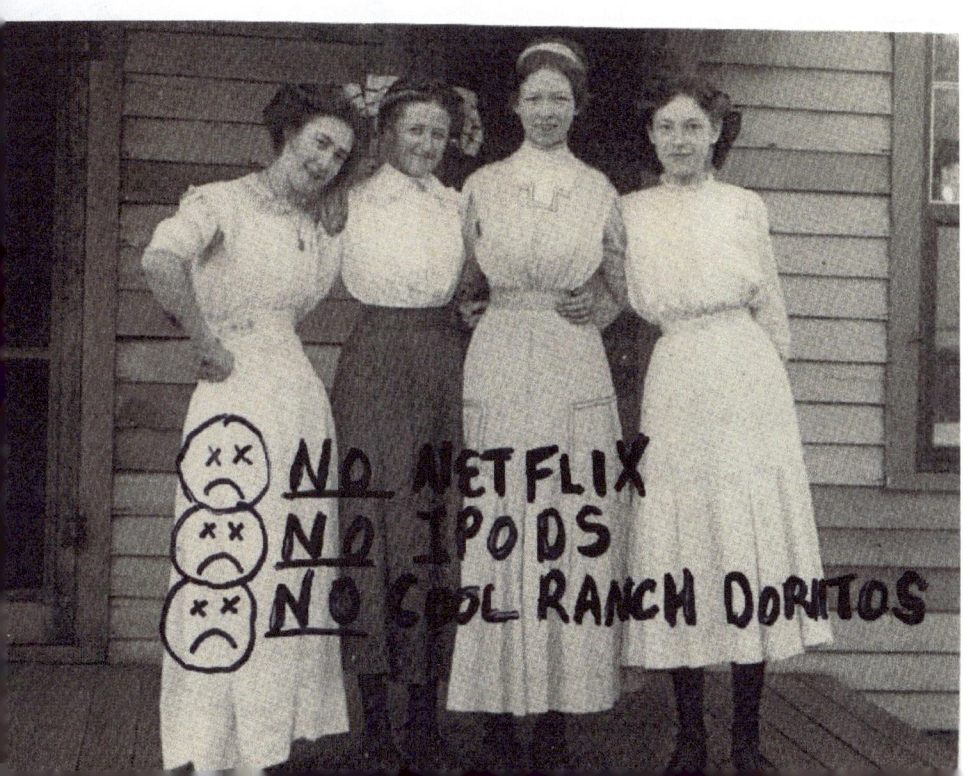

NO NETFLIX
NO IPODS
NO COOL RANCH DORITOS

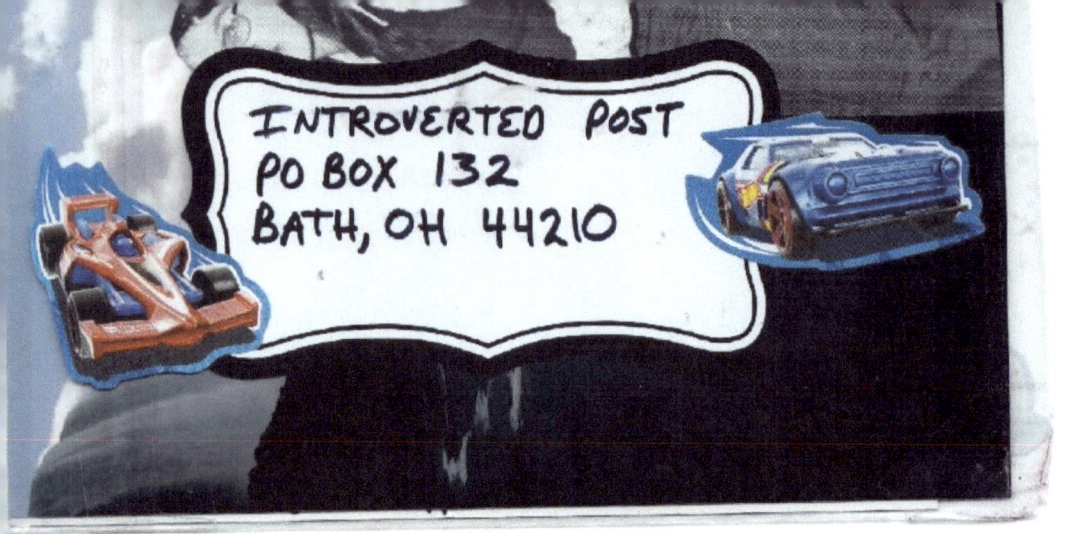

INTROVERTED POST
PO BOX 132
BATH, OH 44210

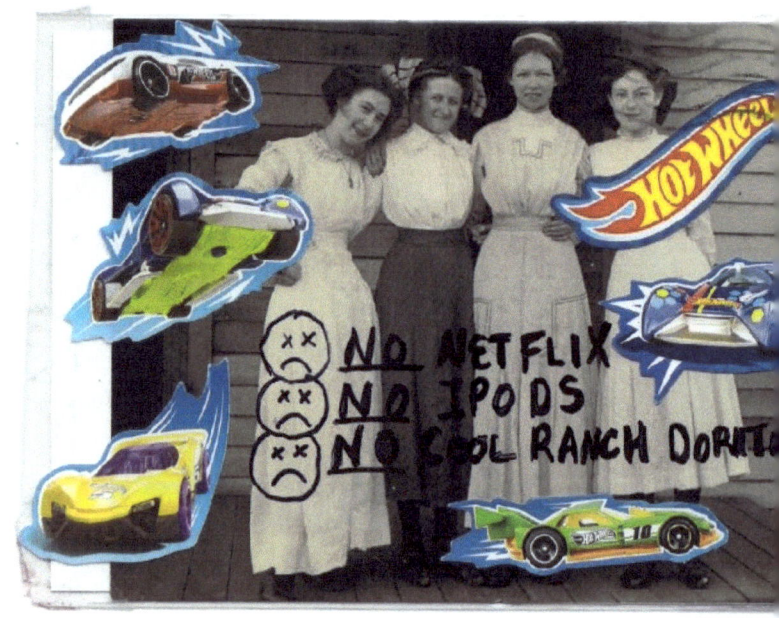

NO NETFLIX
NO IPODS
NO COOL RANCH DORITOS

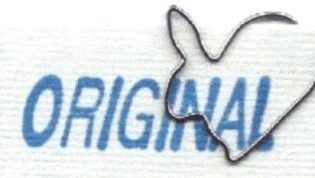

ORIGINAL

THIS
CARD
IS A
REPRINT
OF A
REAL
PHOTO POSTCARD I FOUND
AT A
THRIFT
STORE.
I WONDER
WHAT THESE GIRLS LIVES

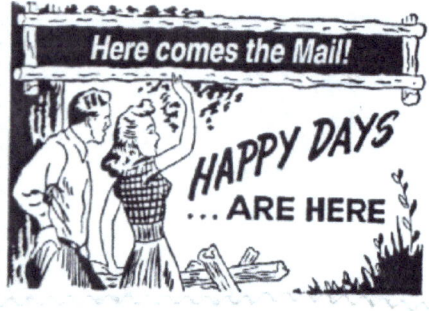

Here comes the Mail!

HAPPY DAYS
...ARE HERE

2019

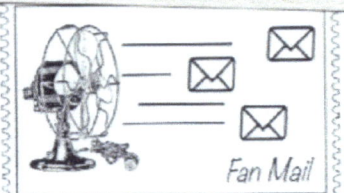

Fan Mail

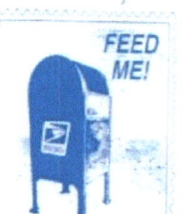

FEED ME!

Fan Mail

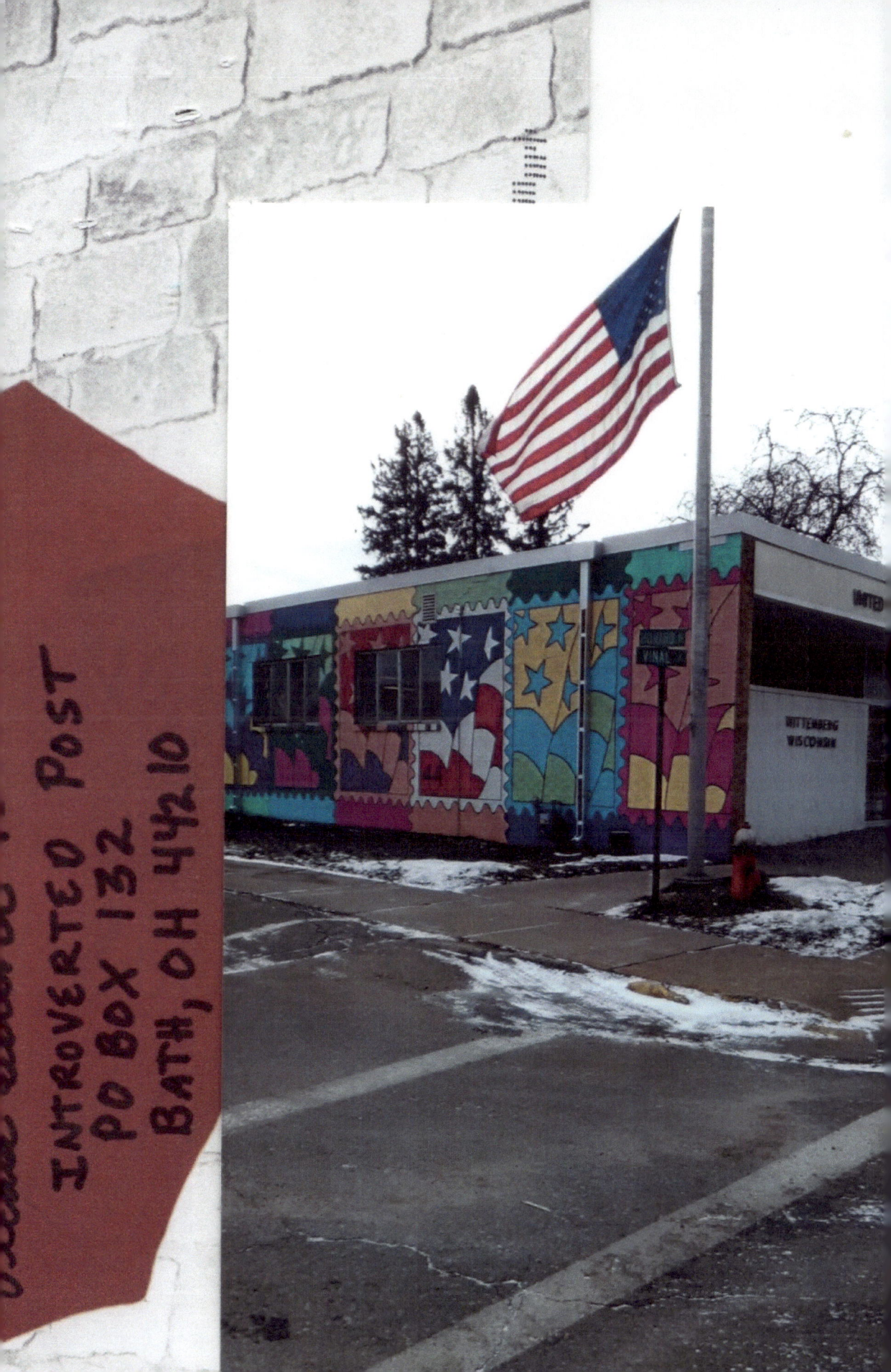

INTROVERTED POST
PO BOX 132
BATH, OH 44210

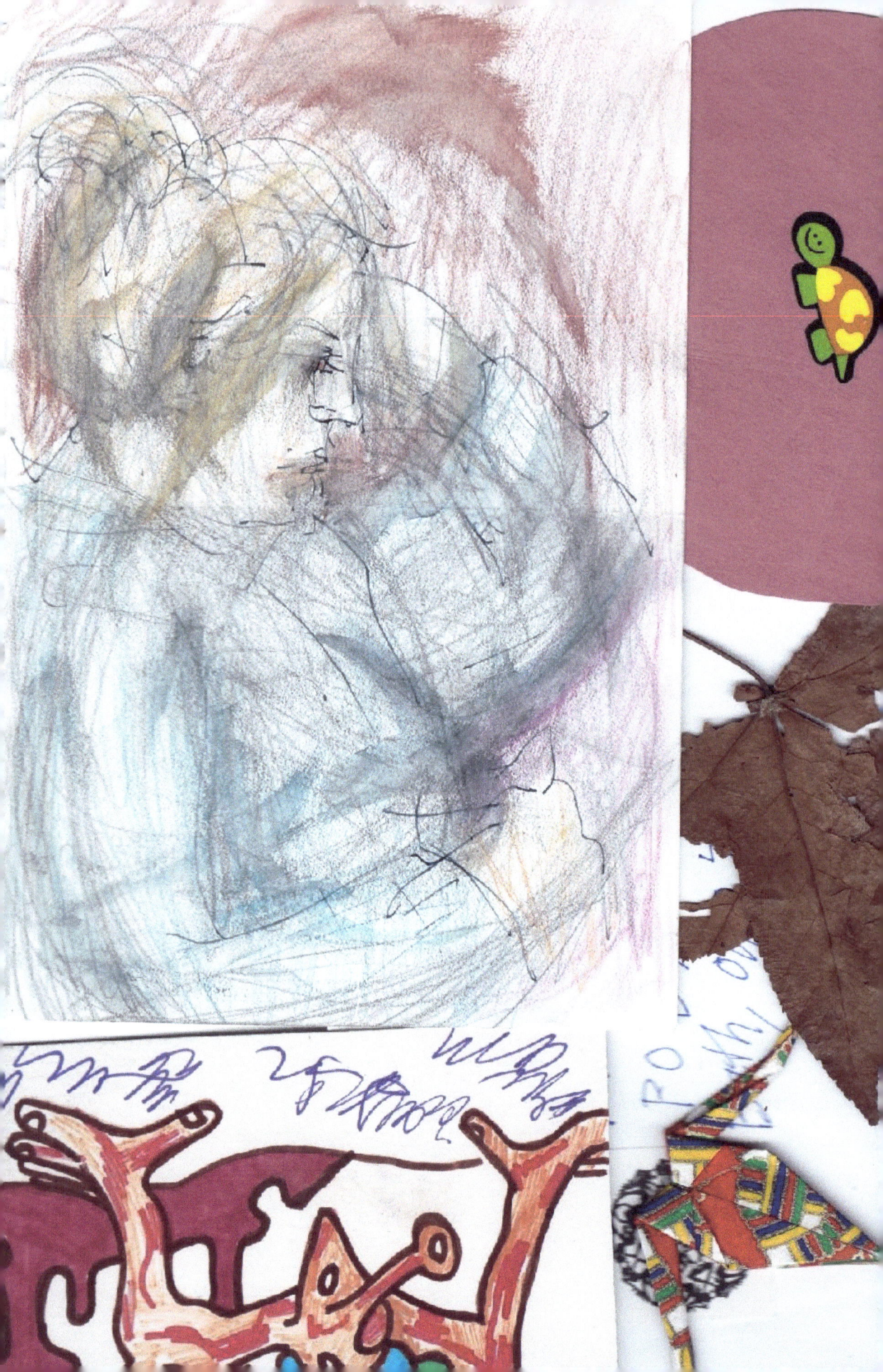

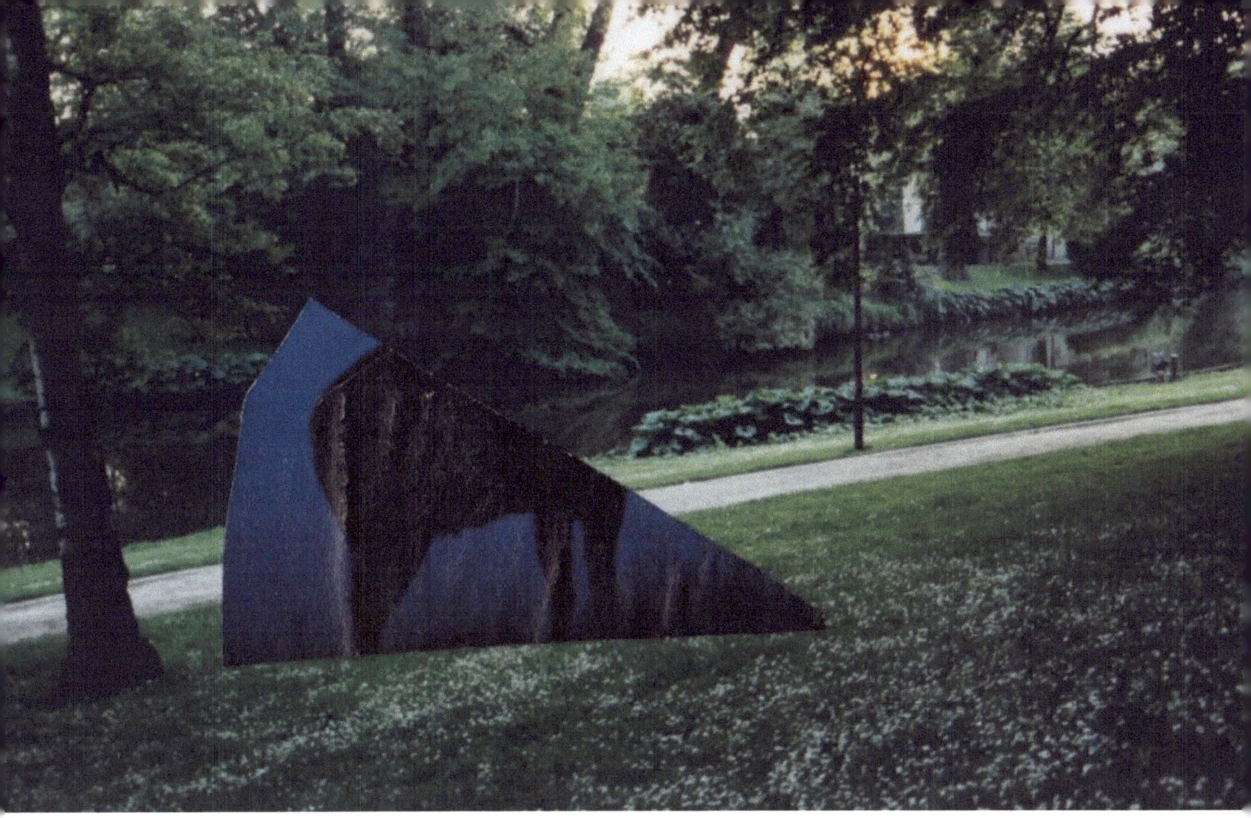

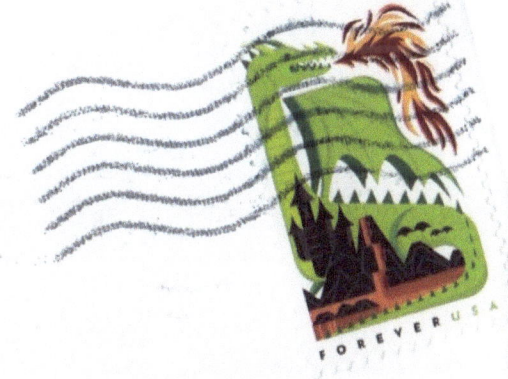

PORTLAND OR 972
01 APR 2019 PM 6 L

FOREVER USA

The Introverted Post
PO Box 132
Bath, Ohio   44210

USA

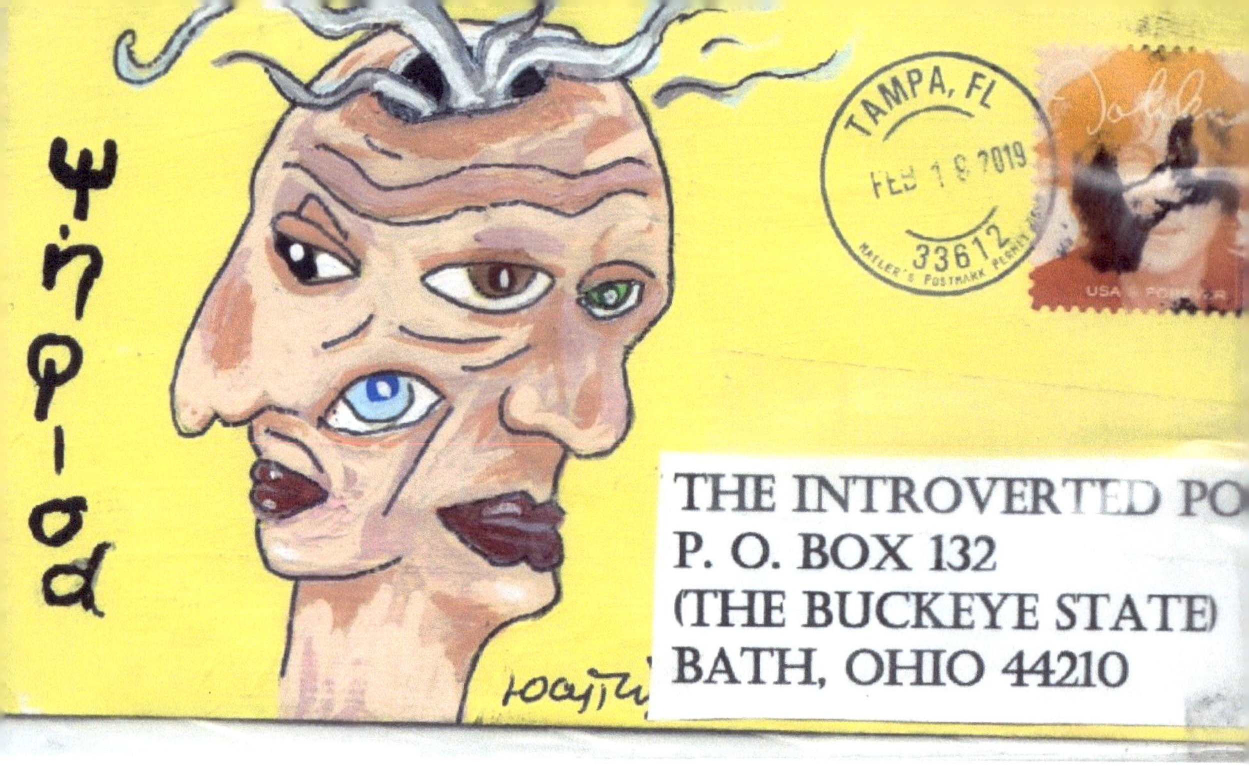

TAMPA, FL
FEB 1 8 2019
33612

THE INTROVERTED PO
P. O. BOX 132
(THE BUCKEYE STATE)
BATH, OHIO 44210

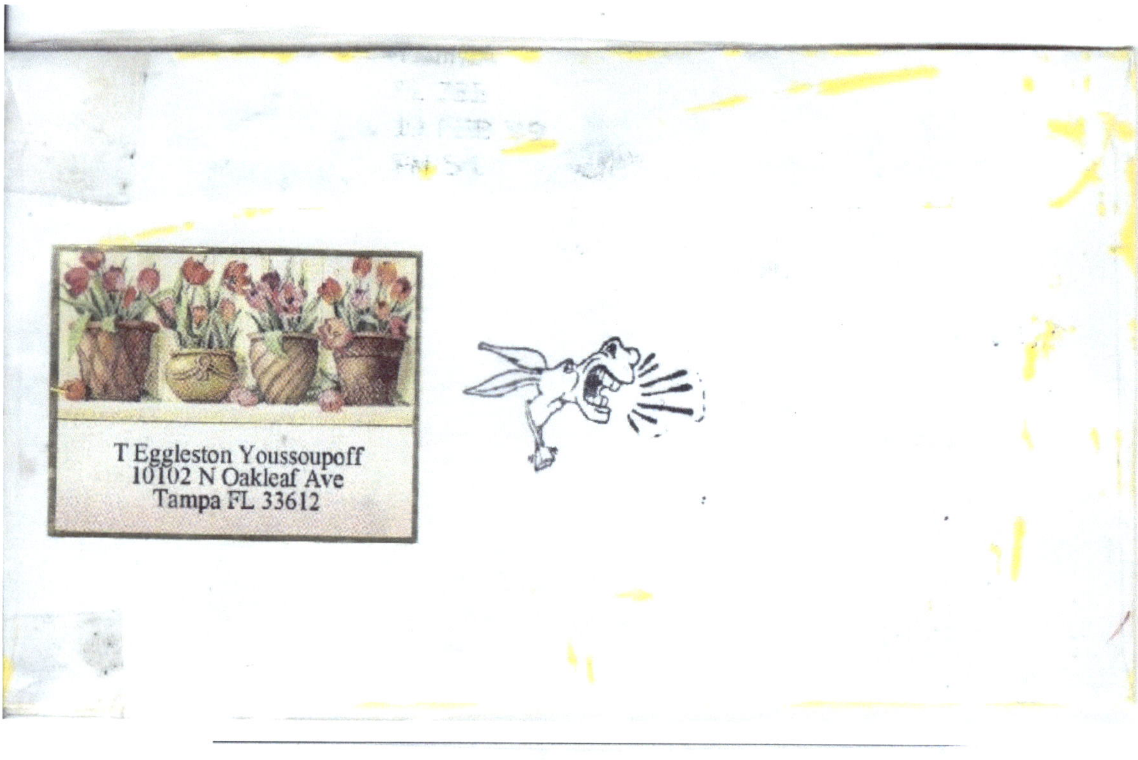

T Eggleston Youssoupoff
10102 N Oakleaf Ave
Tampa FL 33612

COMPLEMENTS AND GREETINGS FROM THE
SWAMPS OF WEST FLORIDA.

MOOI BLY UND PROST

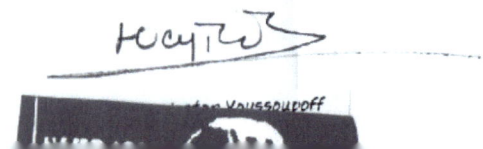

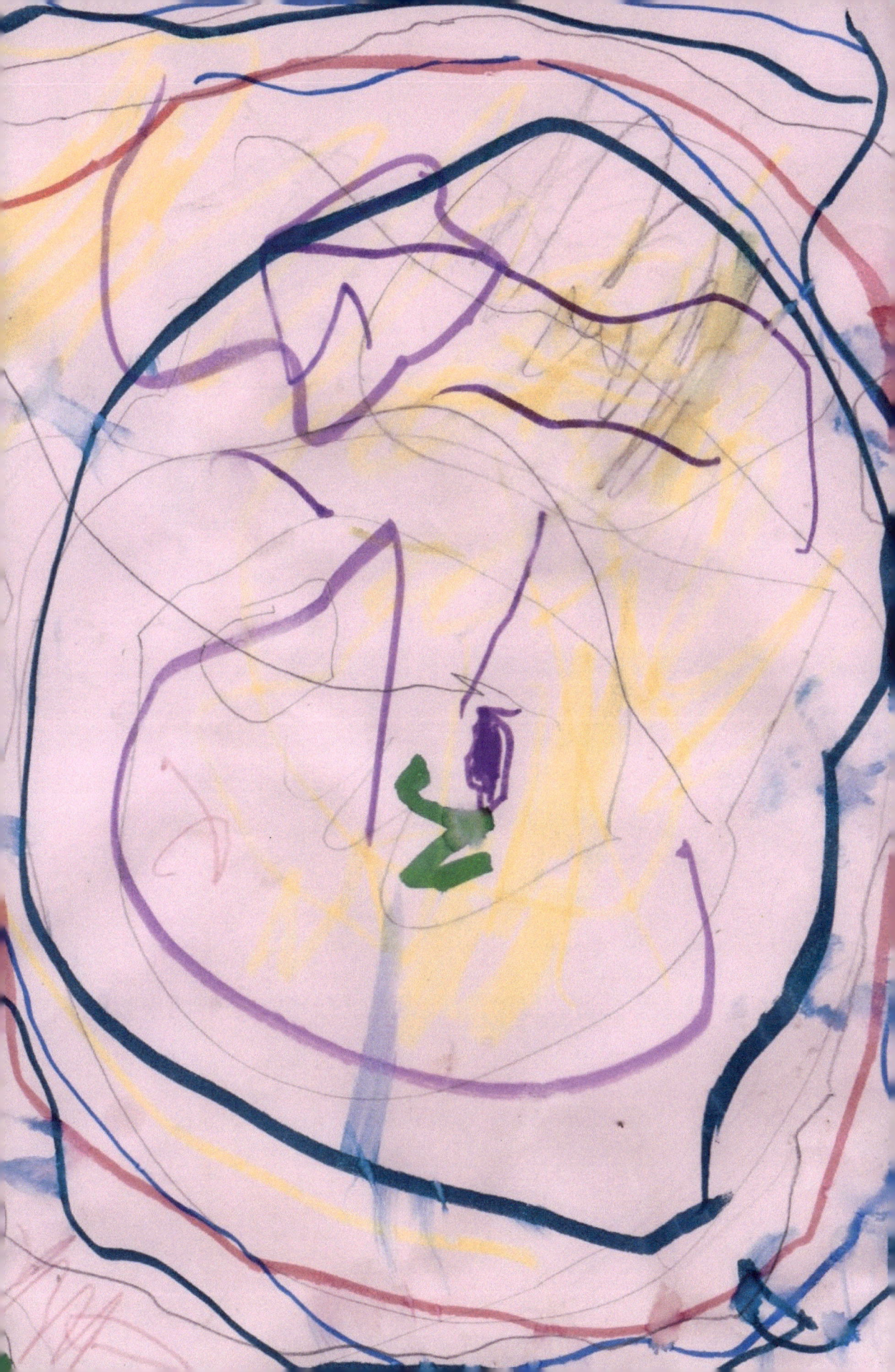

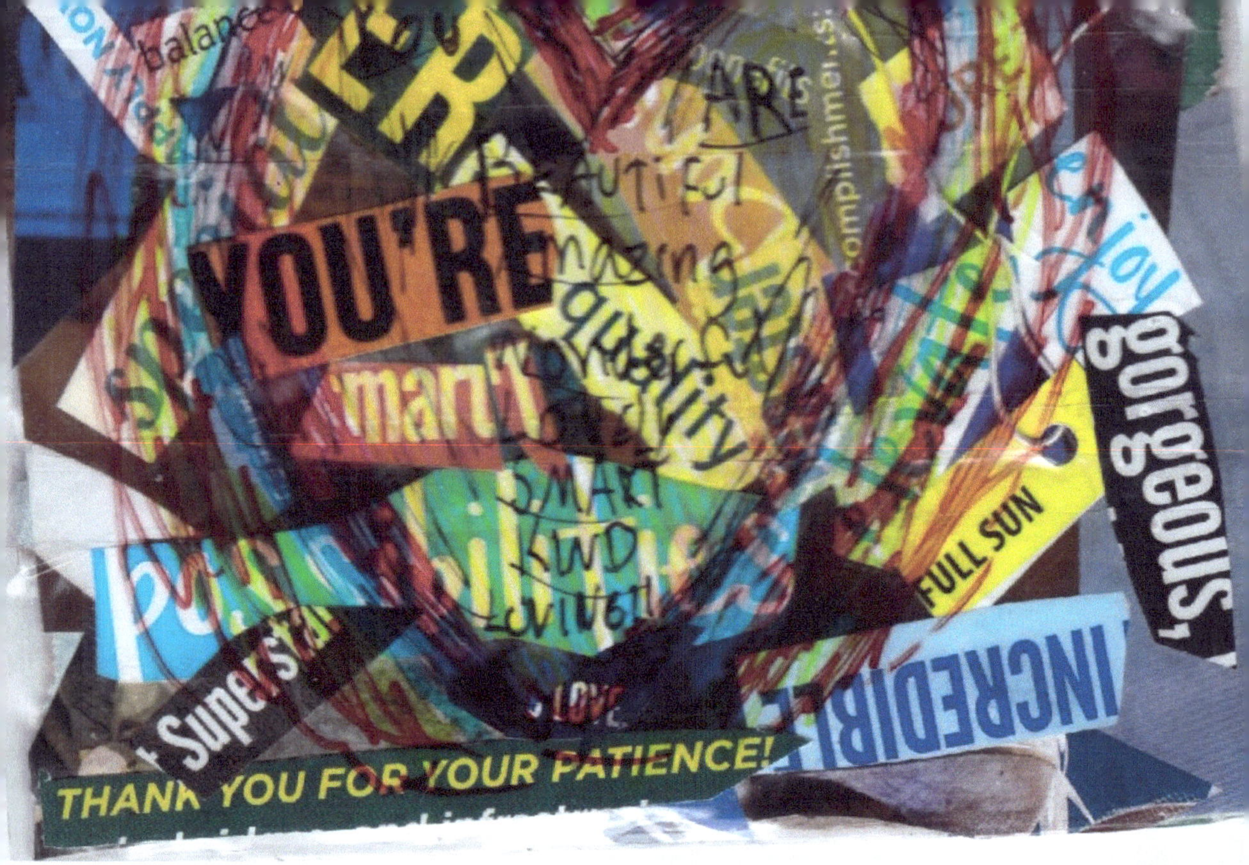

YOU'RE

gorgeous,

smart

beautiful
amazing

FULL SUN

INCREDIBLE

THANK YOU FOR YOUR PATIENCE!

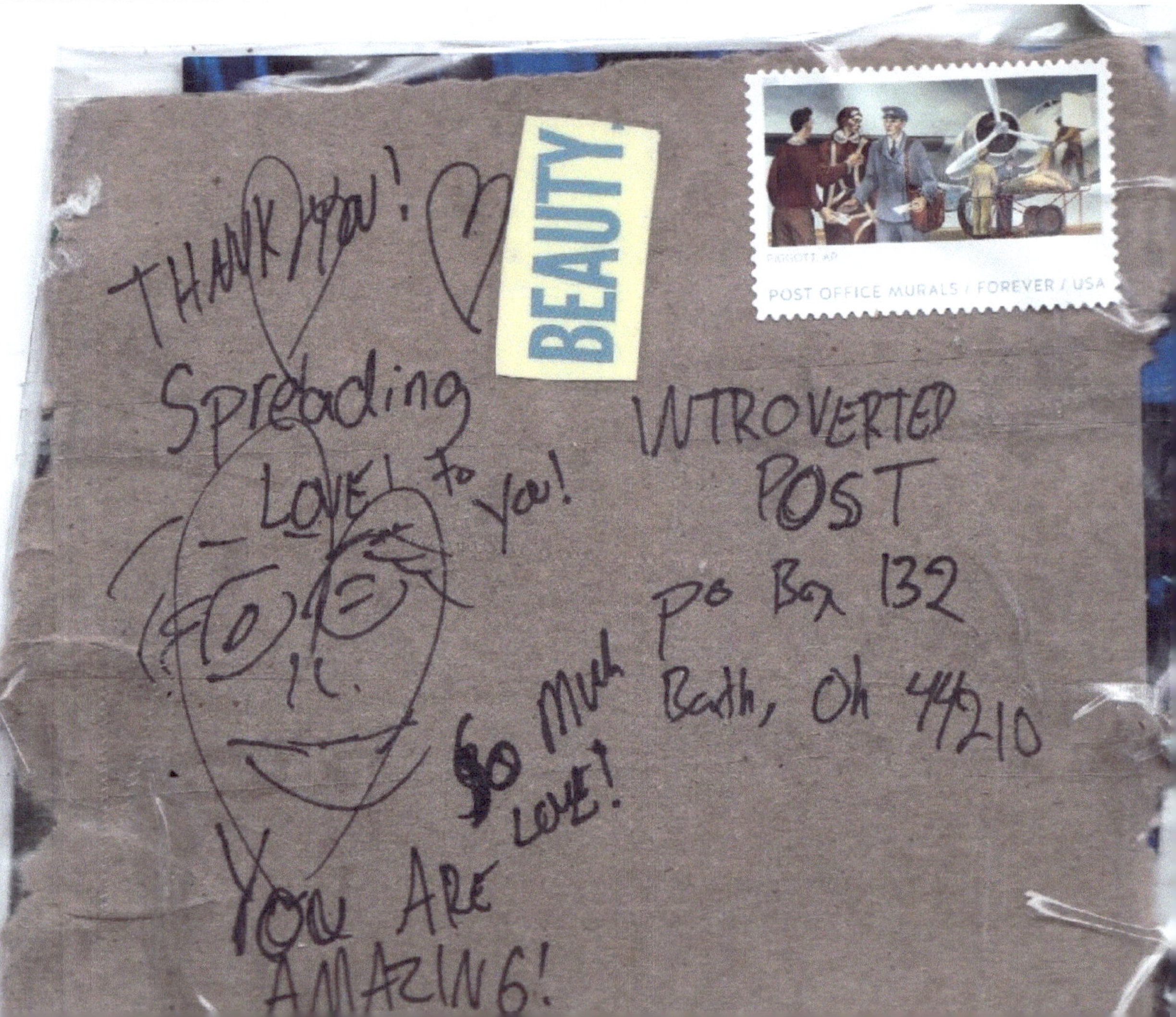

Superstar

LOVE

BEAUTY!

THANK you! ♡

Spreading

LOVE! to you!

So Much
LOVE!

YOU ARE
AMAZING!

INTROVERTED
POST
po Box 132
Bath, Oh 44210

POST OFFICE MURALS / FOREVER / USA

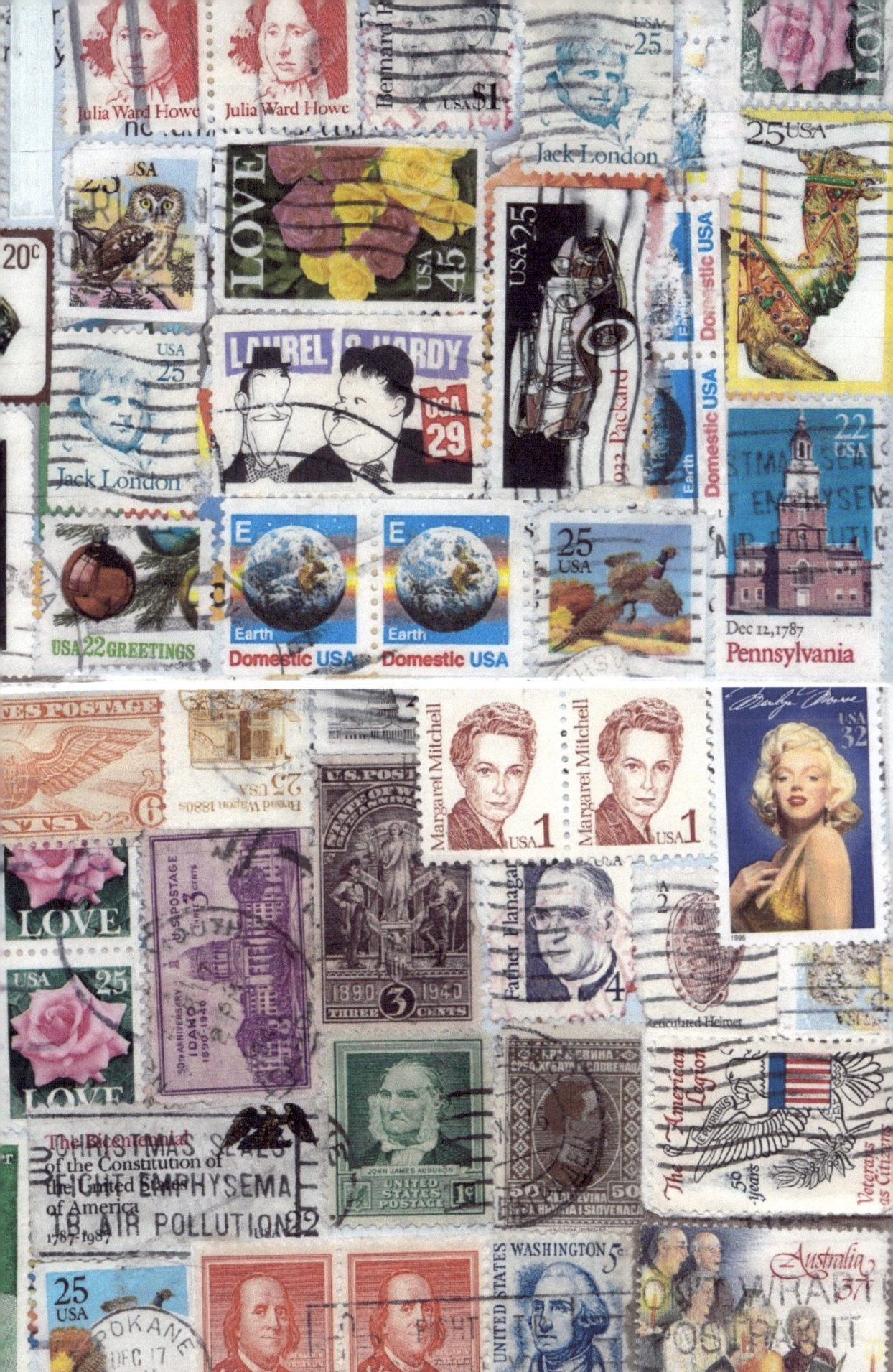

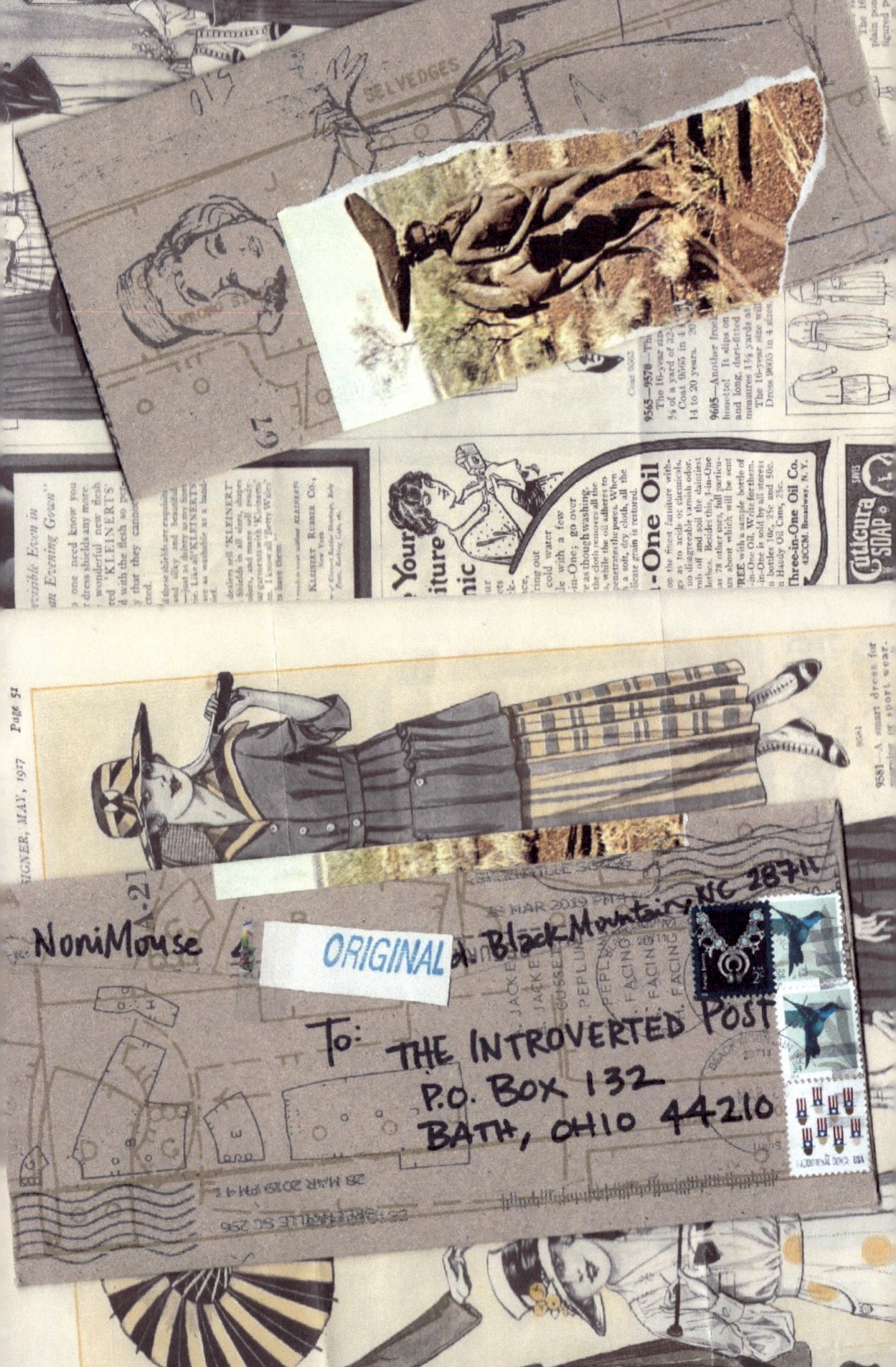

NoniMouse

ORIGINAL at Black Mountain, NC 28711

To: THE INTROVERTED POST
P.O. BOX 132
BATH, OHIO 44210

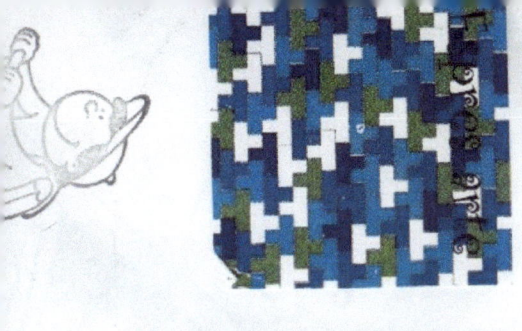

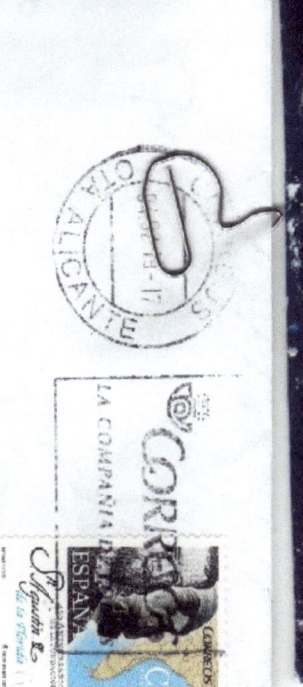

The Introverted Post
P.O. Box 132
Bath, Ohio 44210

CORREOS
LA COMPAÑIA DE...
ESPANA

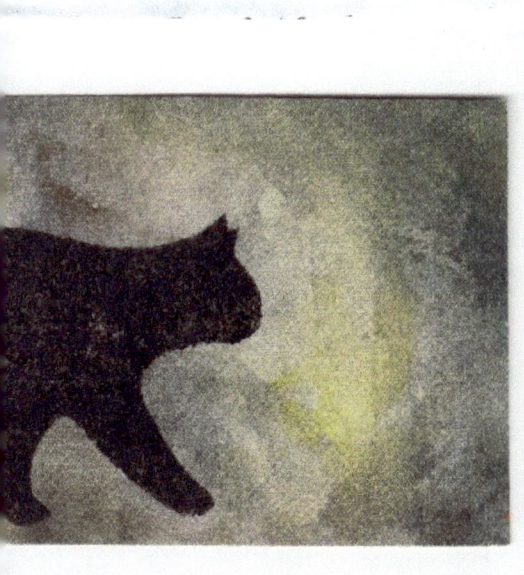

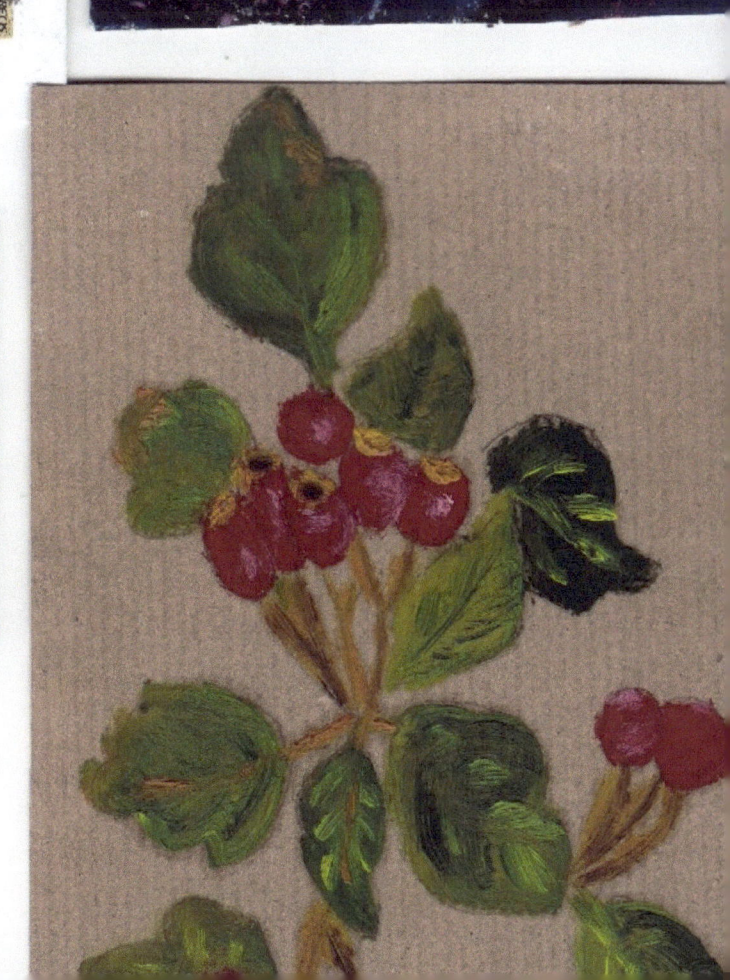

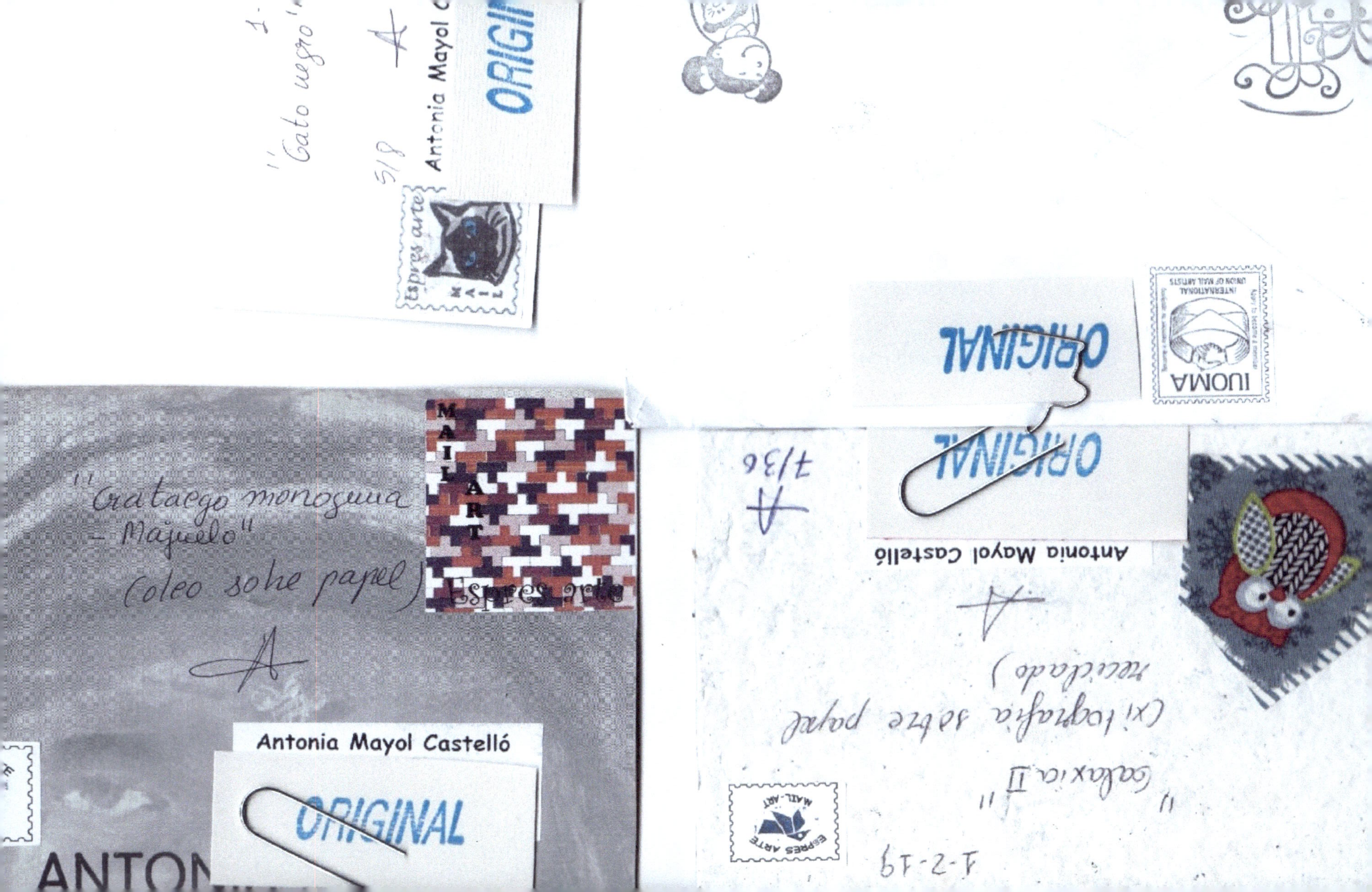

ANTON

Antonia Mayol Castelló

"Crataego monogena
– Majuelo"
(óleo sobre papel)

ITALIA

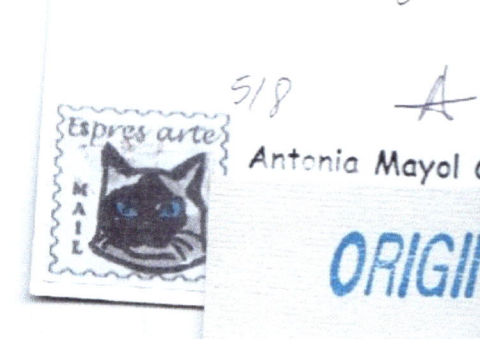

1.
"Gato negro"

5/8

Antonia Mayol C

Espres arte
MAIL

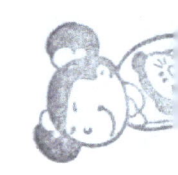

ESPRES ARTE
MAIL ART

7/36

1-2-19

"Galaxia II"
(xilografía sobre papel
reciclado)

Antonia Mayol Castelló

IUOMA
INTERNATIONAL UNION OF MAIL ARTISTS

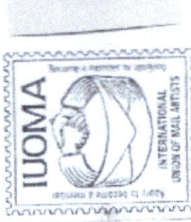

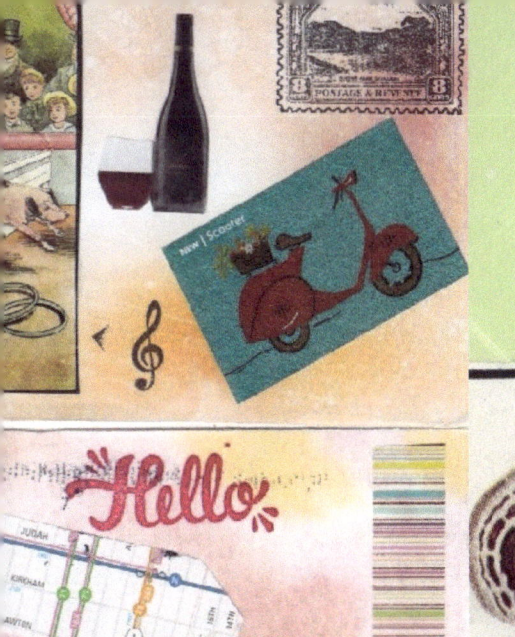

Hello

Paper Dreams

DO SOMETHING CREATIVE EVERY DAY

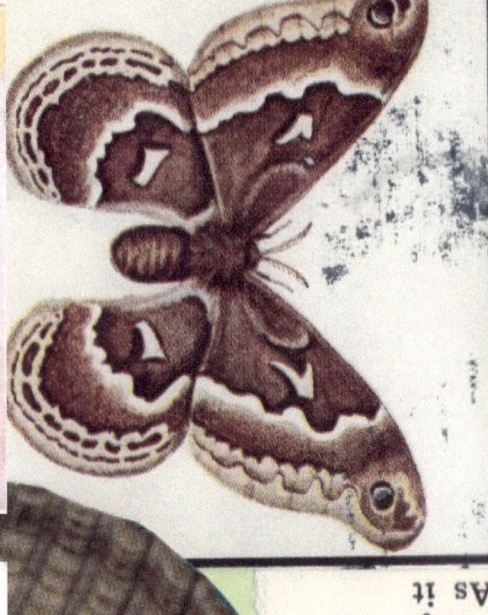

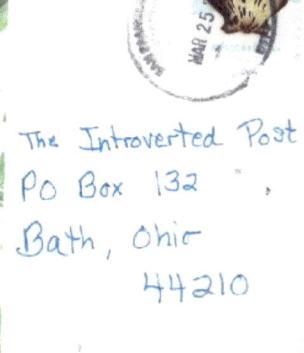

The Introverted Post
PO Box 132
Bath, Ohio
44210

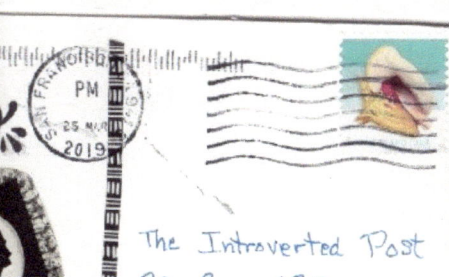

The Introverted Post
PO Box 132
Bath, Ohio
44210

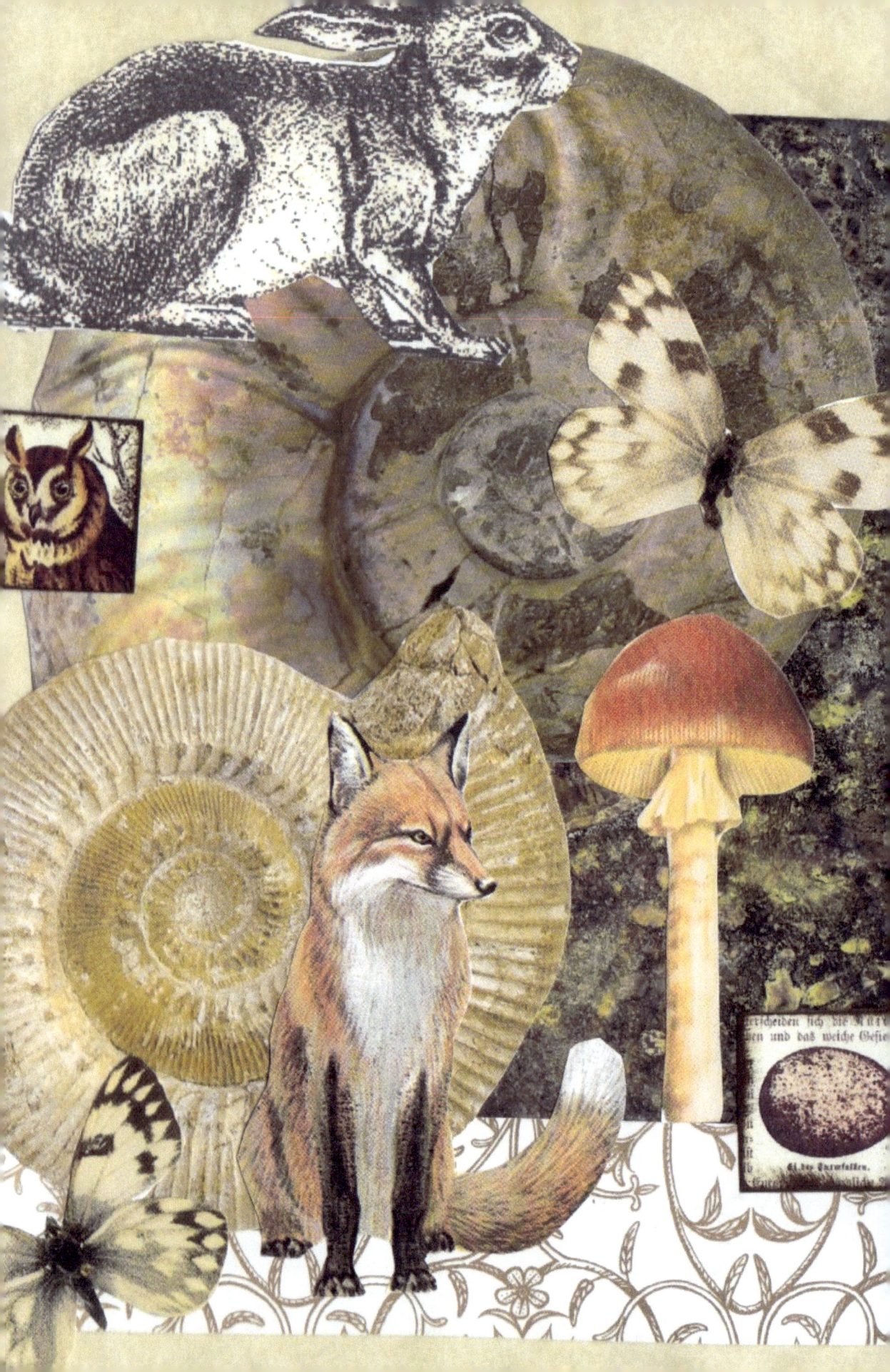

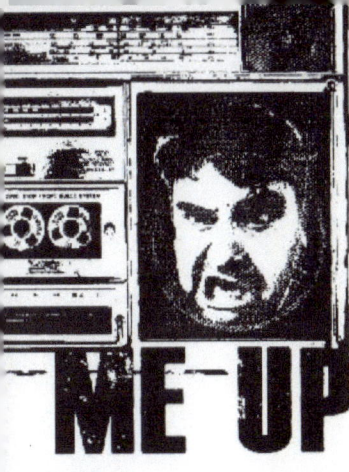

ME UP

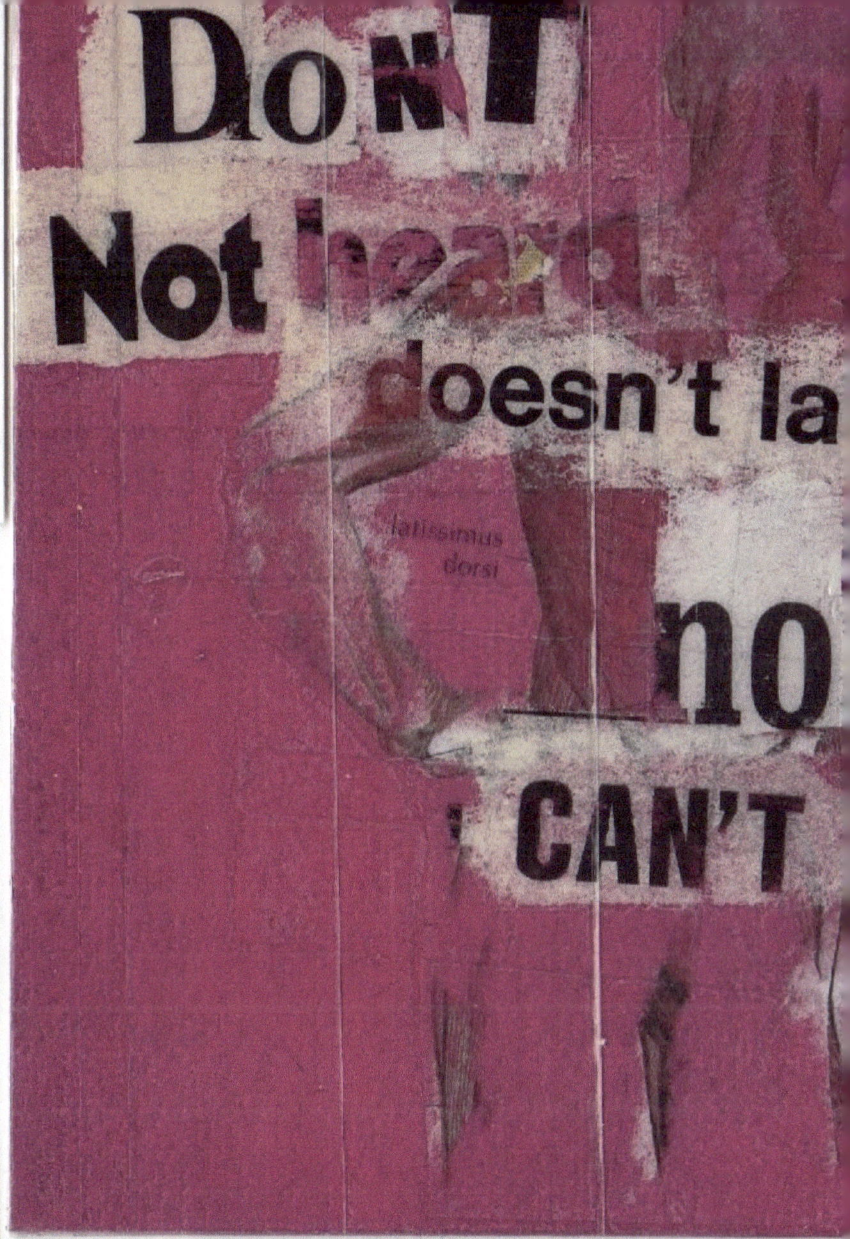

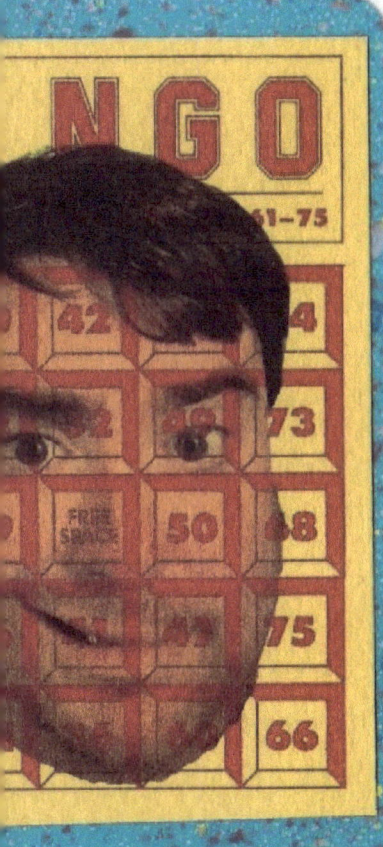

DoN**T**

Not heard.

doesn't la

*latissimus
dorsi*

no

CAN'T

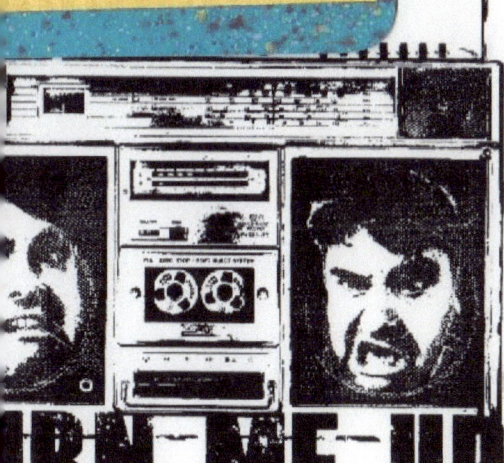

RN ME UP

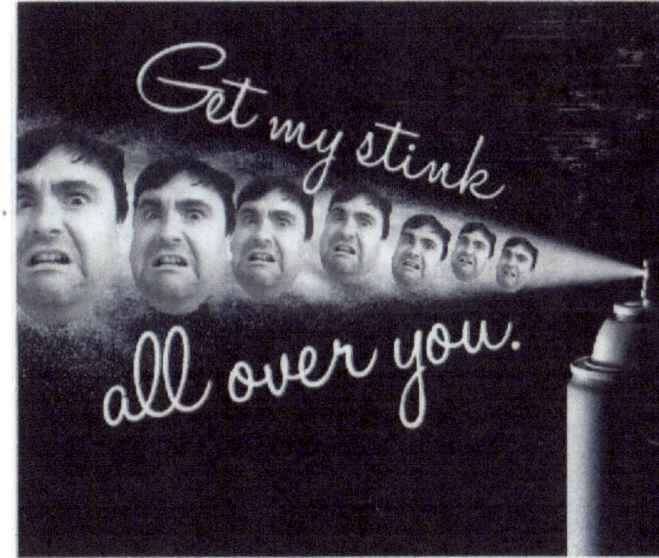

Get my stink

all over you.

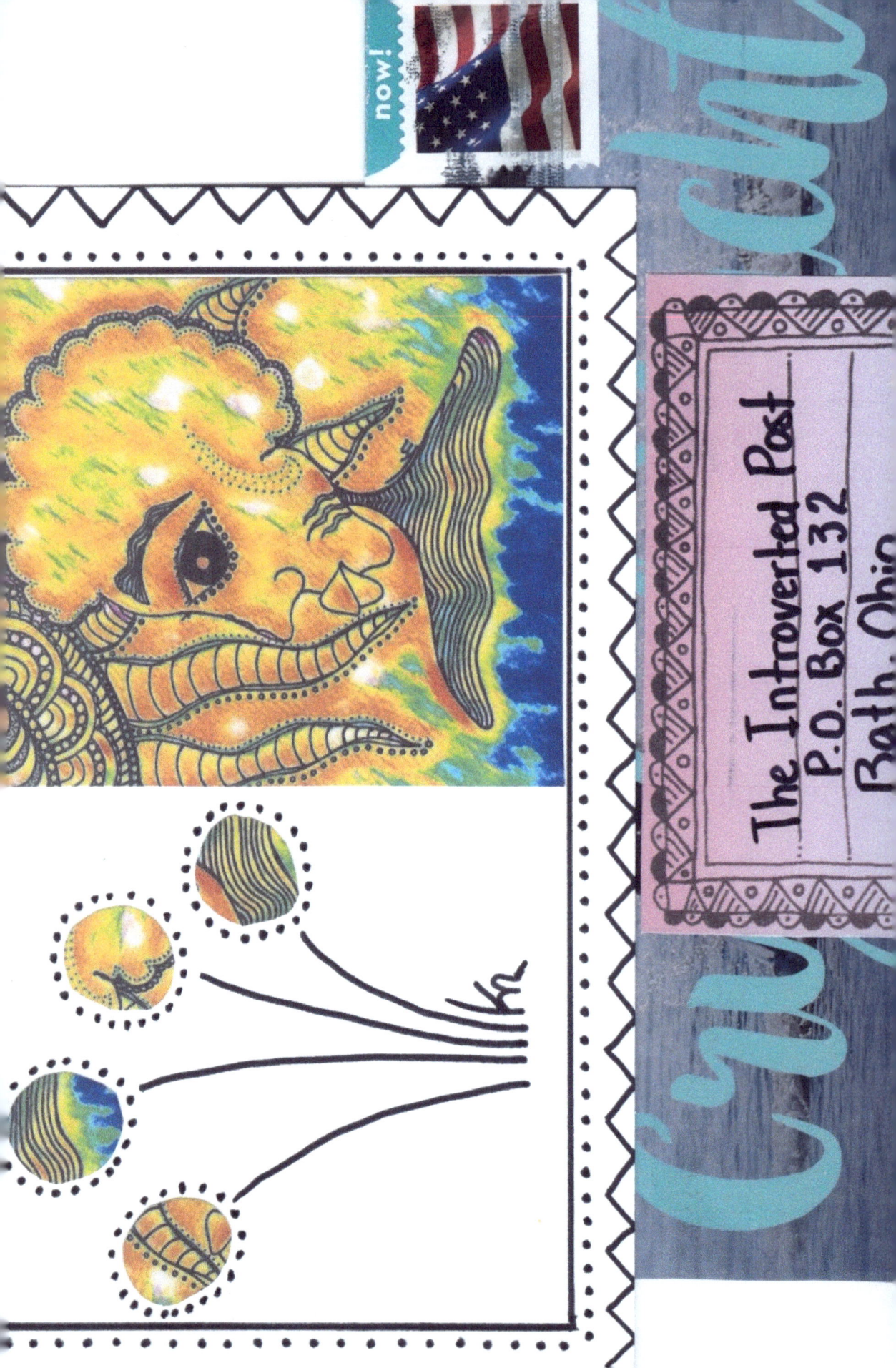

now!

The Introverted Post
P.O. Box 132
Bath, Ohio

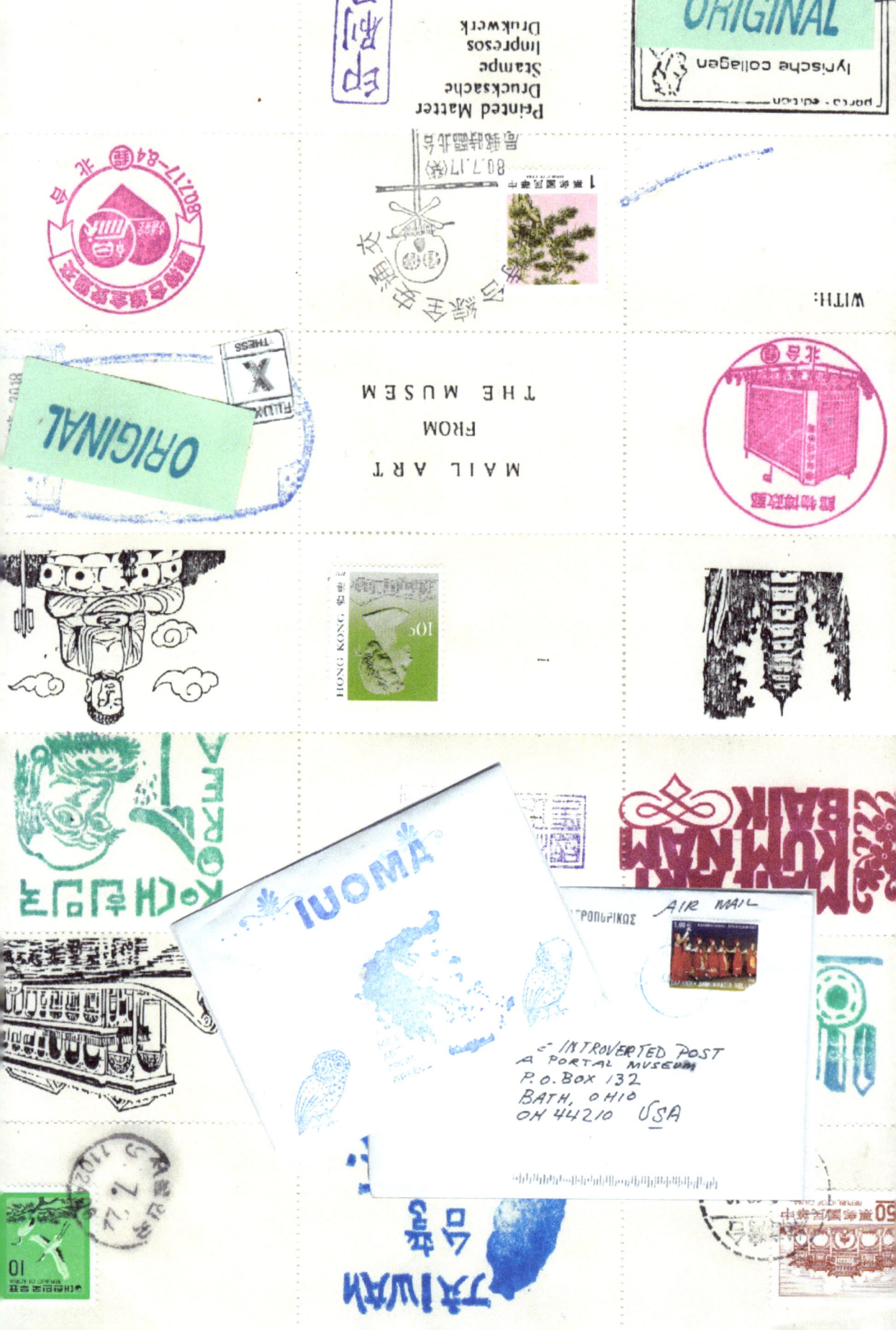

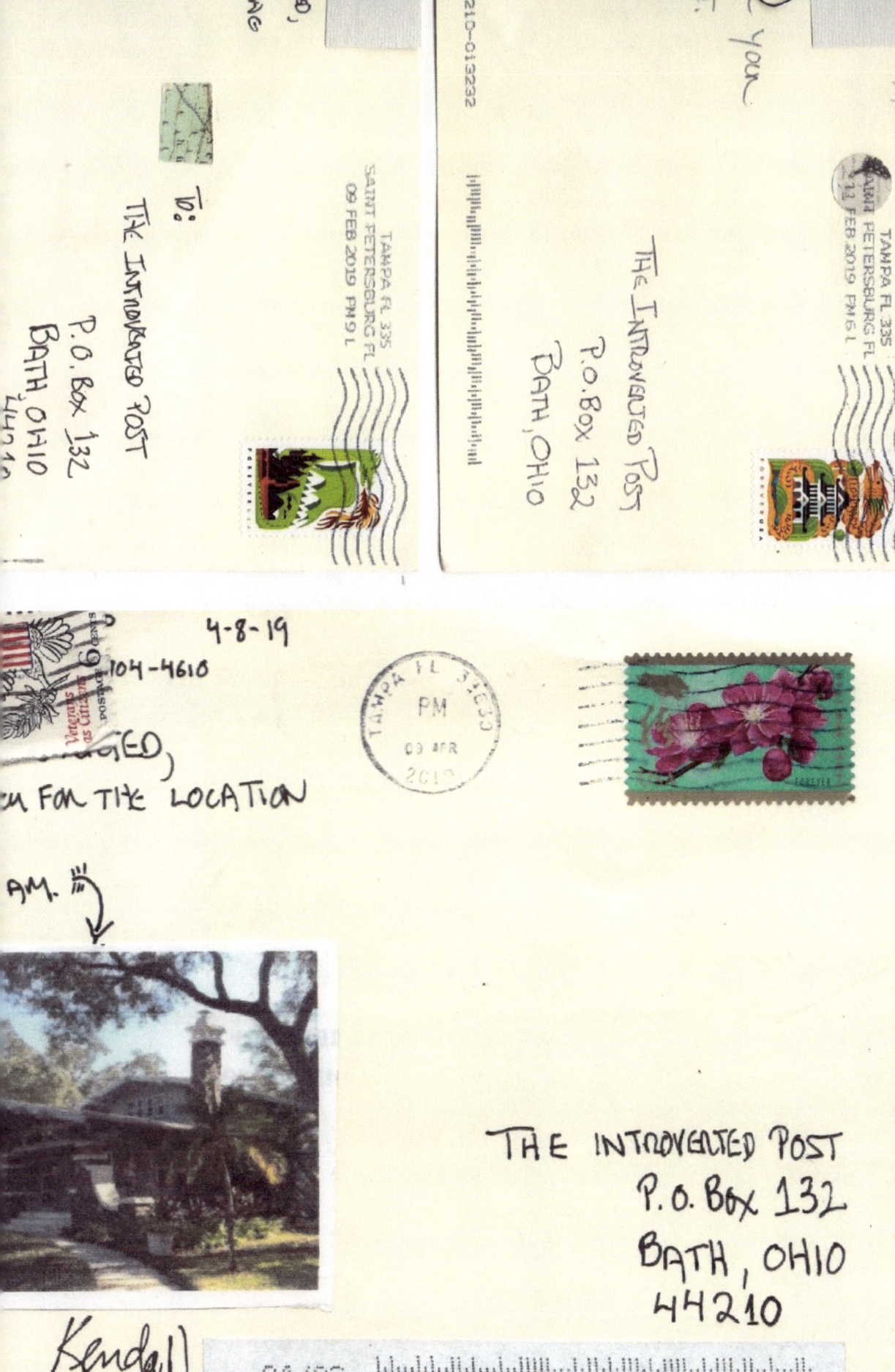

2/11/2019

you

...10-013232

TAMPA FL 335
SAINT PETERSBURG FL
09 FEB 2019 PM 9 L

THE INTROVERTED POST
P.O. Box 132
BATH, OHIO

To:

THE INTROVERTED POST
P.O. Box 132
BATH, OHIO
44210

TAMPA PETERSBURG FL
11 FEB 2019 PM 6 L

TAMPA FL 335

THE INTROVERTED POST
P.O. Box 132
BATH, OHIO

4-8-19
104-4610

...ED)

...u FOR THE LOCATION

A.M.

TAMPA FL 33633
PM
09 APR
2019

THE INTROVERTED POST
P.O. Box 132
BATH, OHIO
44210

Kendall

04/09

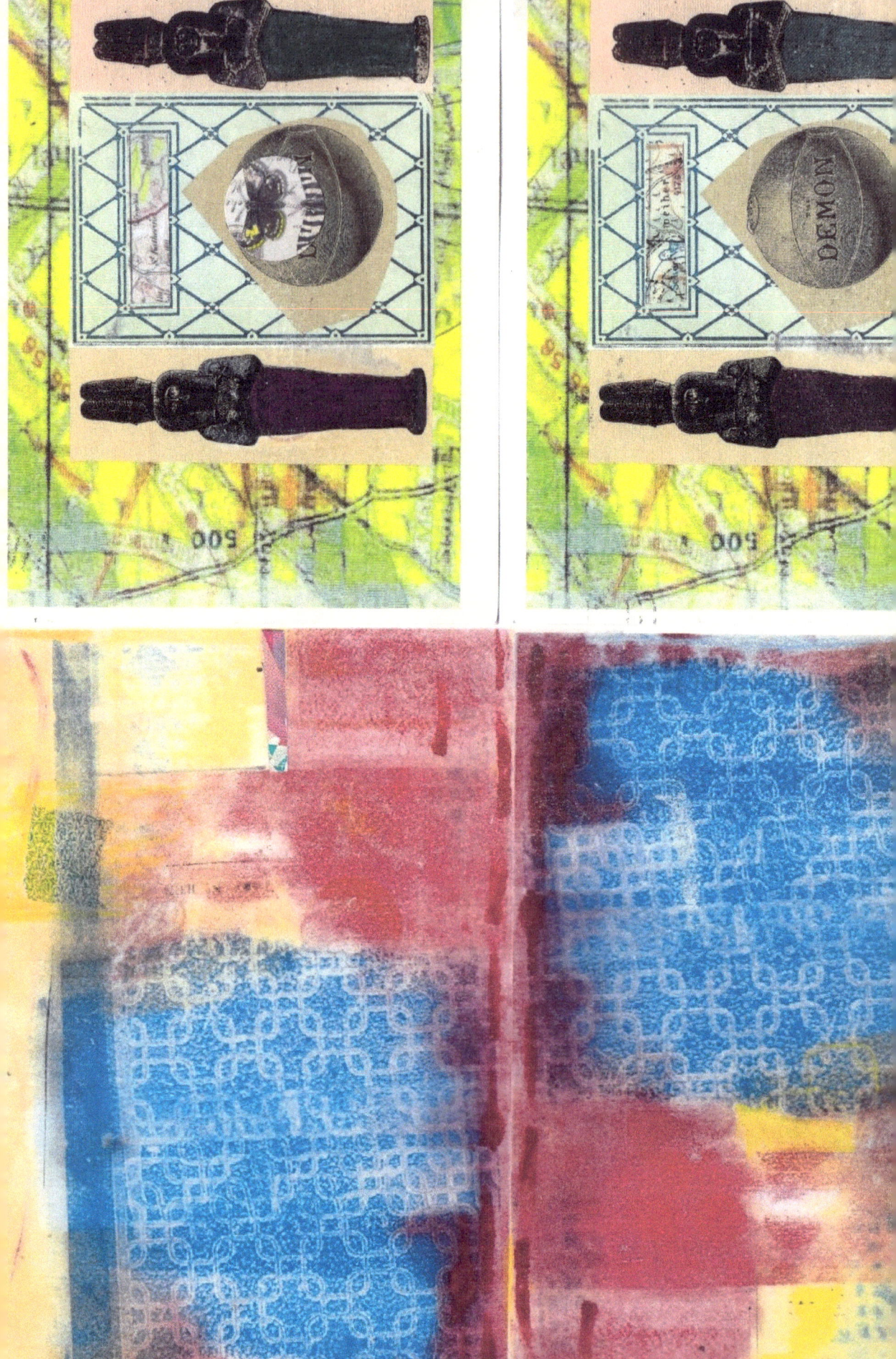

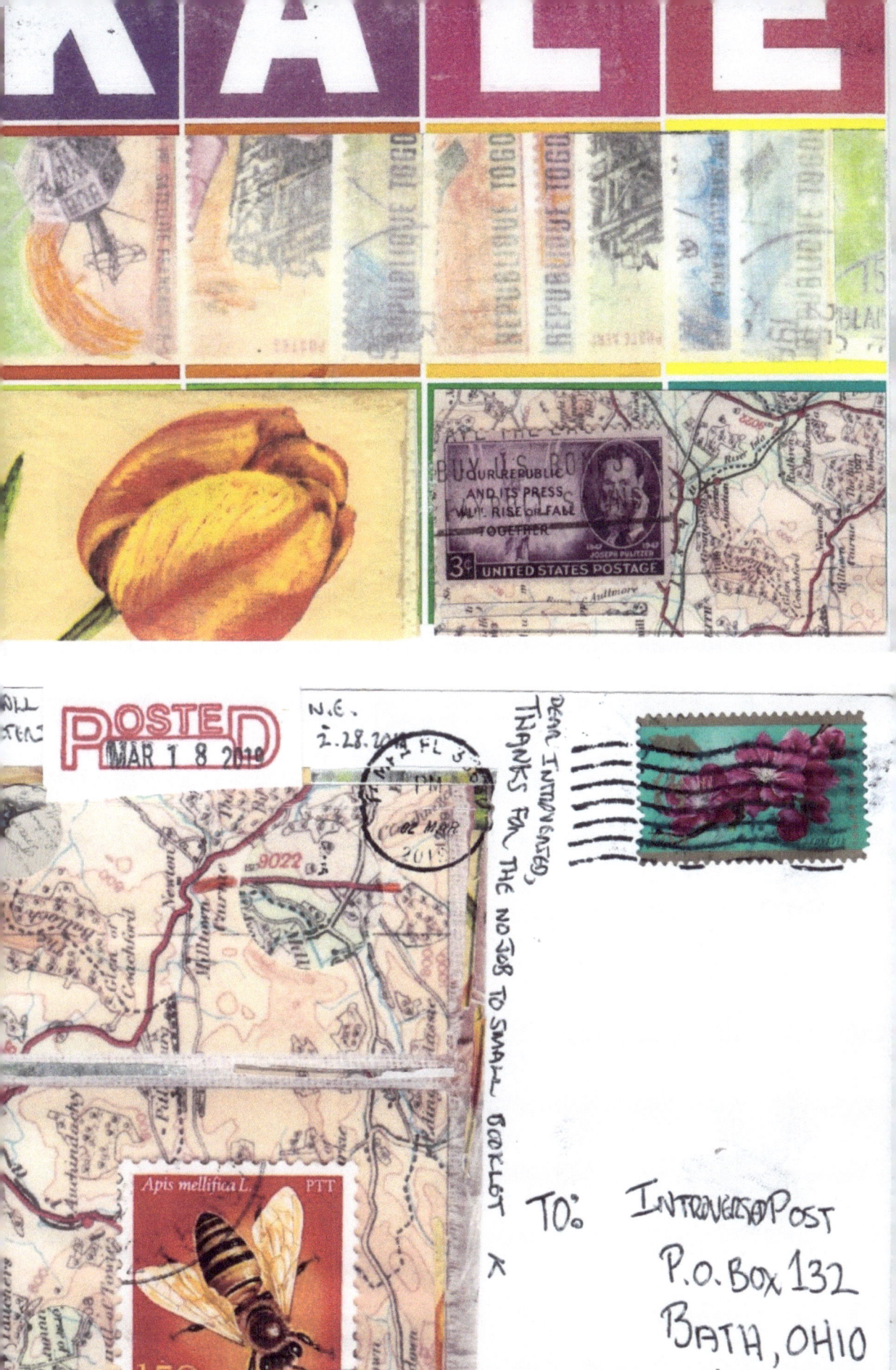

KALE

BUY U.S.
OUR REPUBLIC
AND ITS PRESS
WILL RISE OR FALL
TOGETHER
JOSEPH PULITZER
1847 1947
3¢ UNITED STATES POSTAGE

POSTED
MAR 18 2019

N.E.
2.28.2019

DEAR INTROVERTED,
THANKS FOR THE NO JOB TO SMALL BOOKLET K

TO: INTROVERT@POST
P.O.BOX 132
BATH, OHIO

Apis mellifica L.   PTT
150

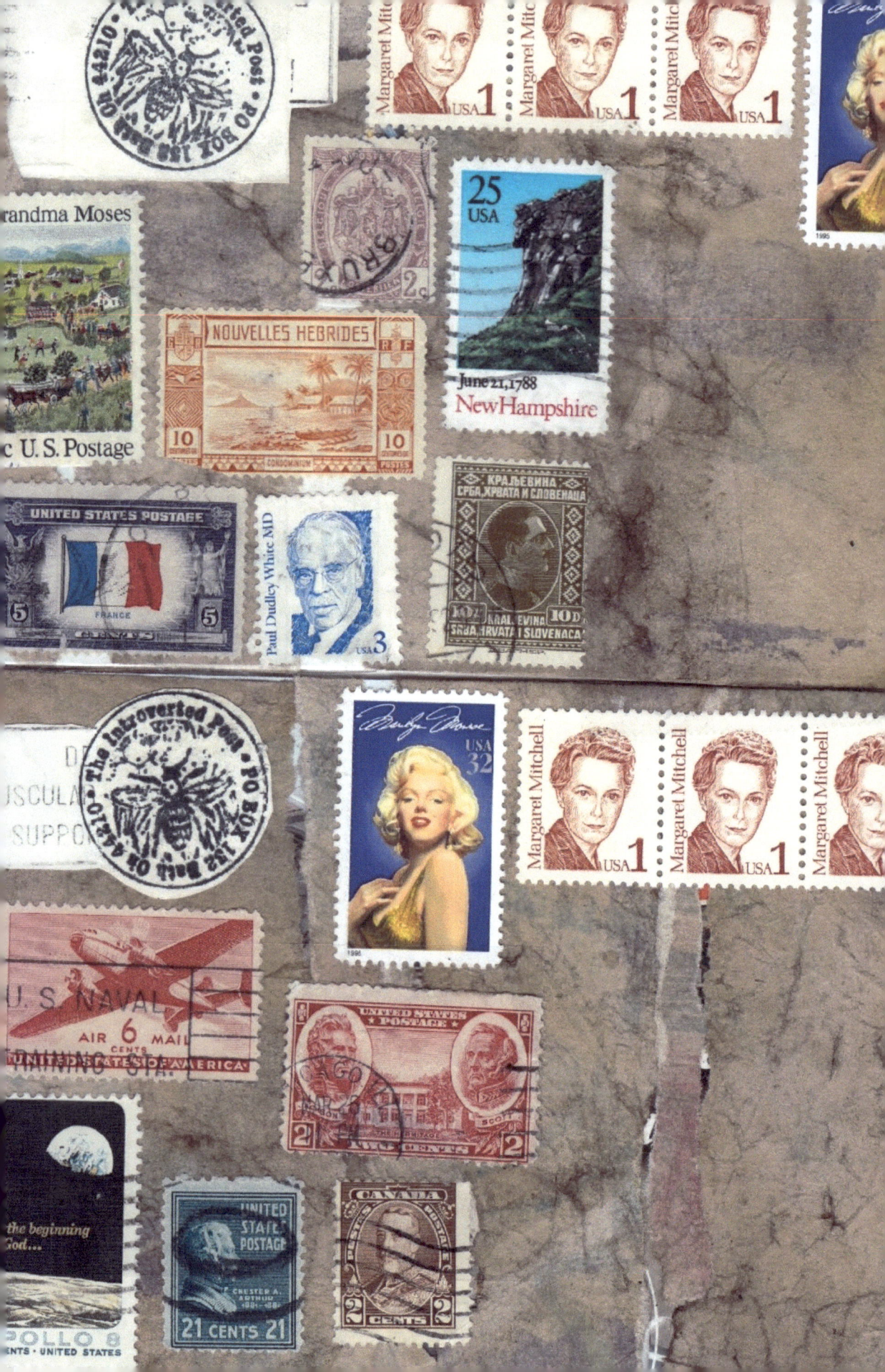

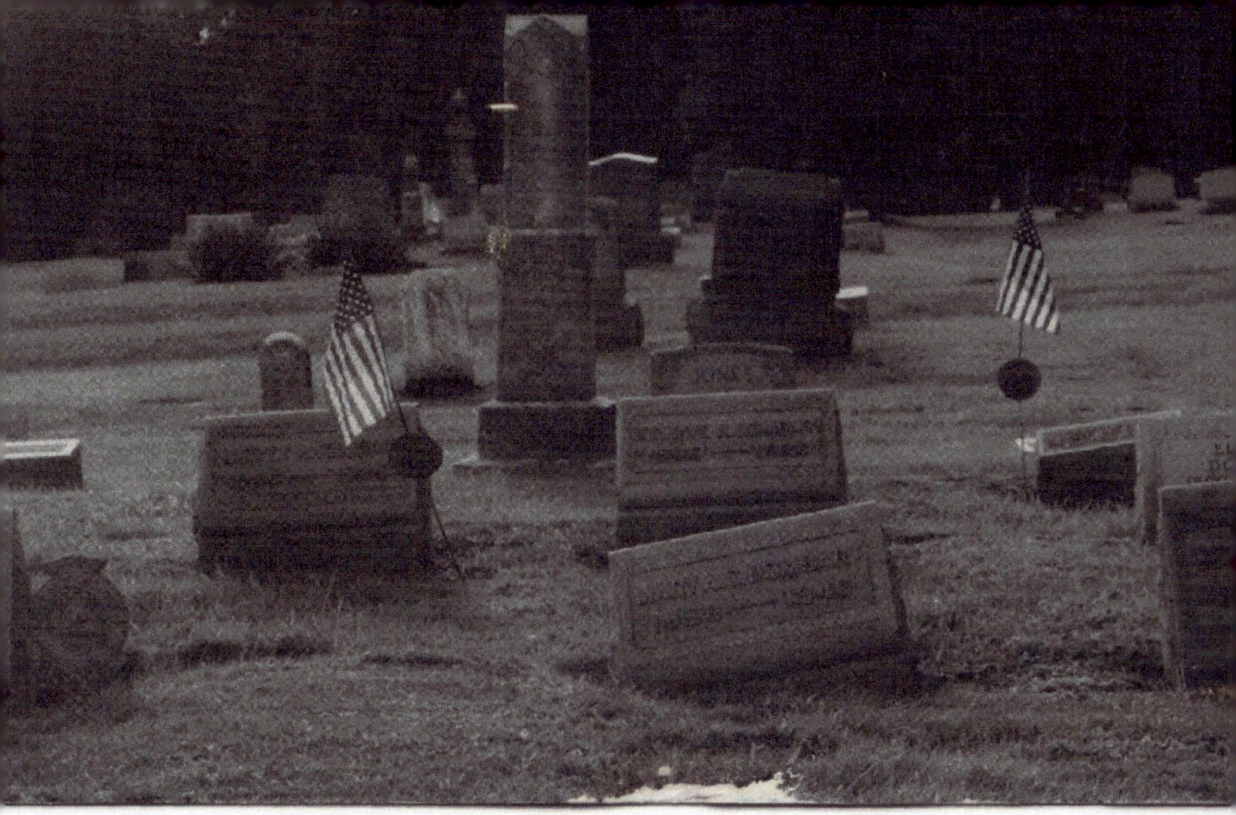

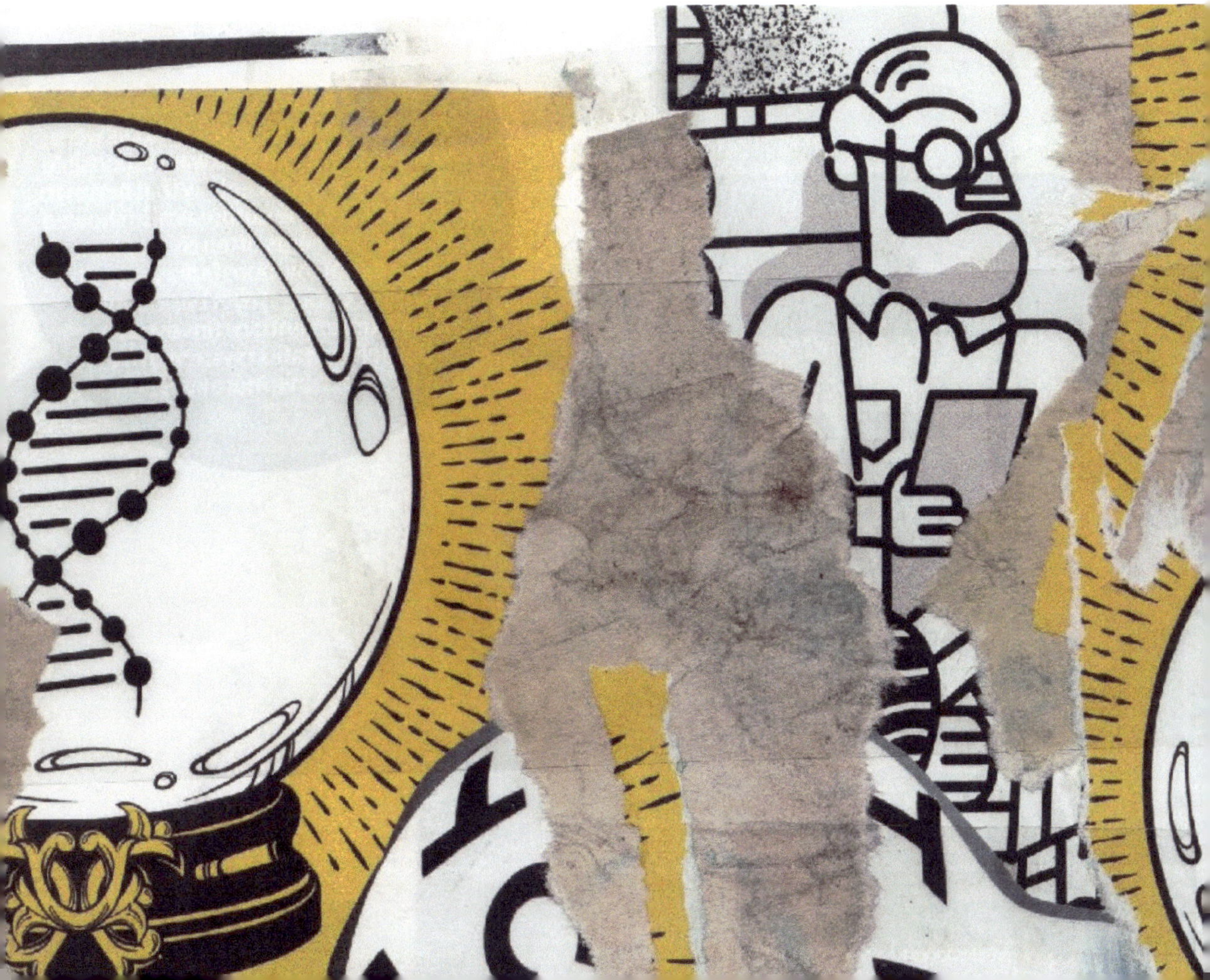

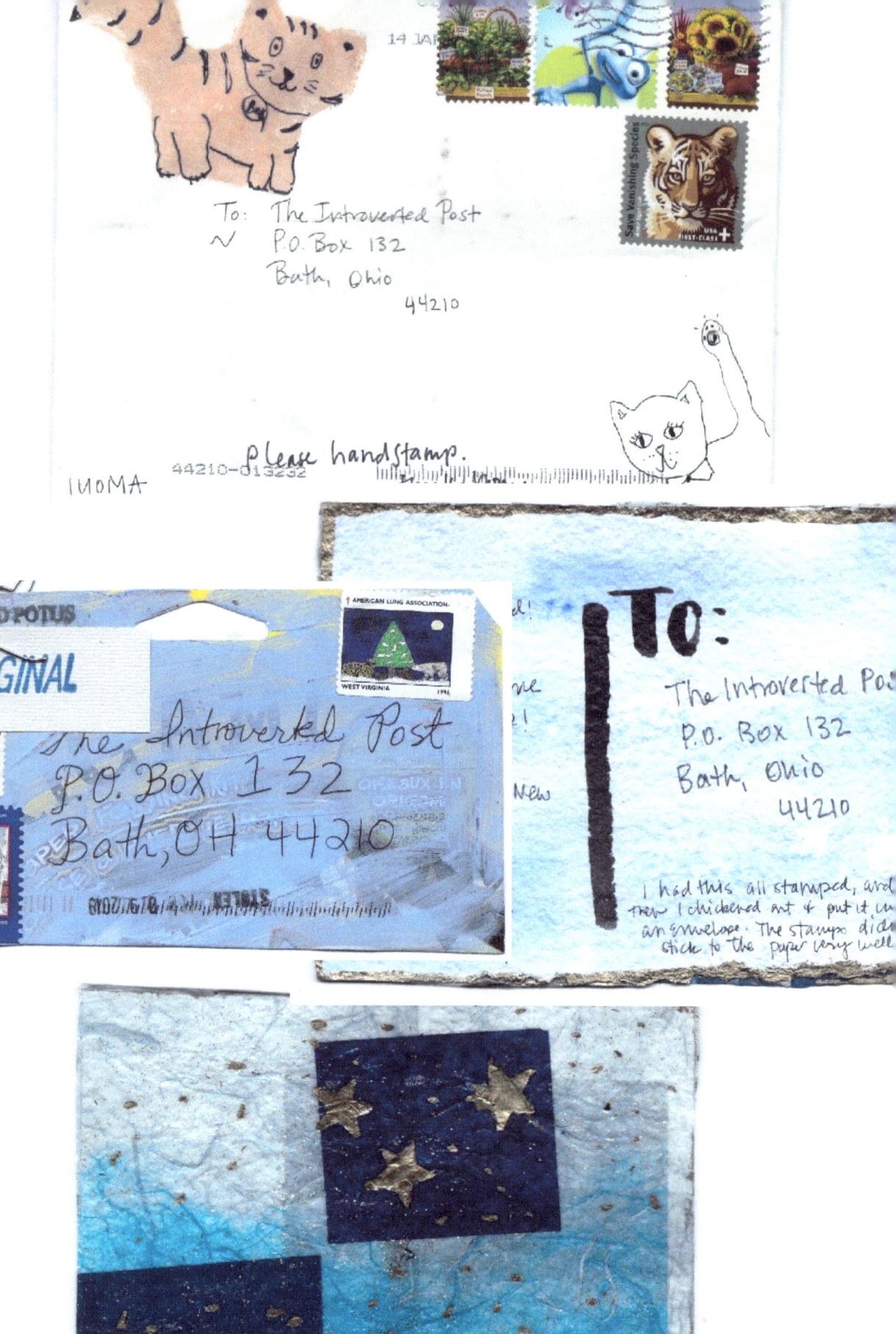

To: The Introverted Post
P.O. Box 132
Bath, Ohio
44210

Please handstamp.

IИOMA   44210-013232

D POTUS
GINAL

↑ AMERICAN LUNG ASSOCIATION.
WEST VIRGINIA   1996

The Introverted Post
P.O. Box 132
Bath, OH 44210

To:

The Introverted Post
P.O. Box 132
Bath, Ohio
44210

I had this all stamped, and
then I chickened out & put it in
an envelope. The stamps didn't
stick to the paper very well

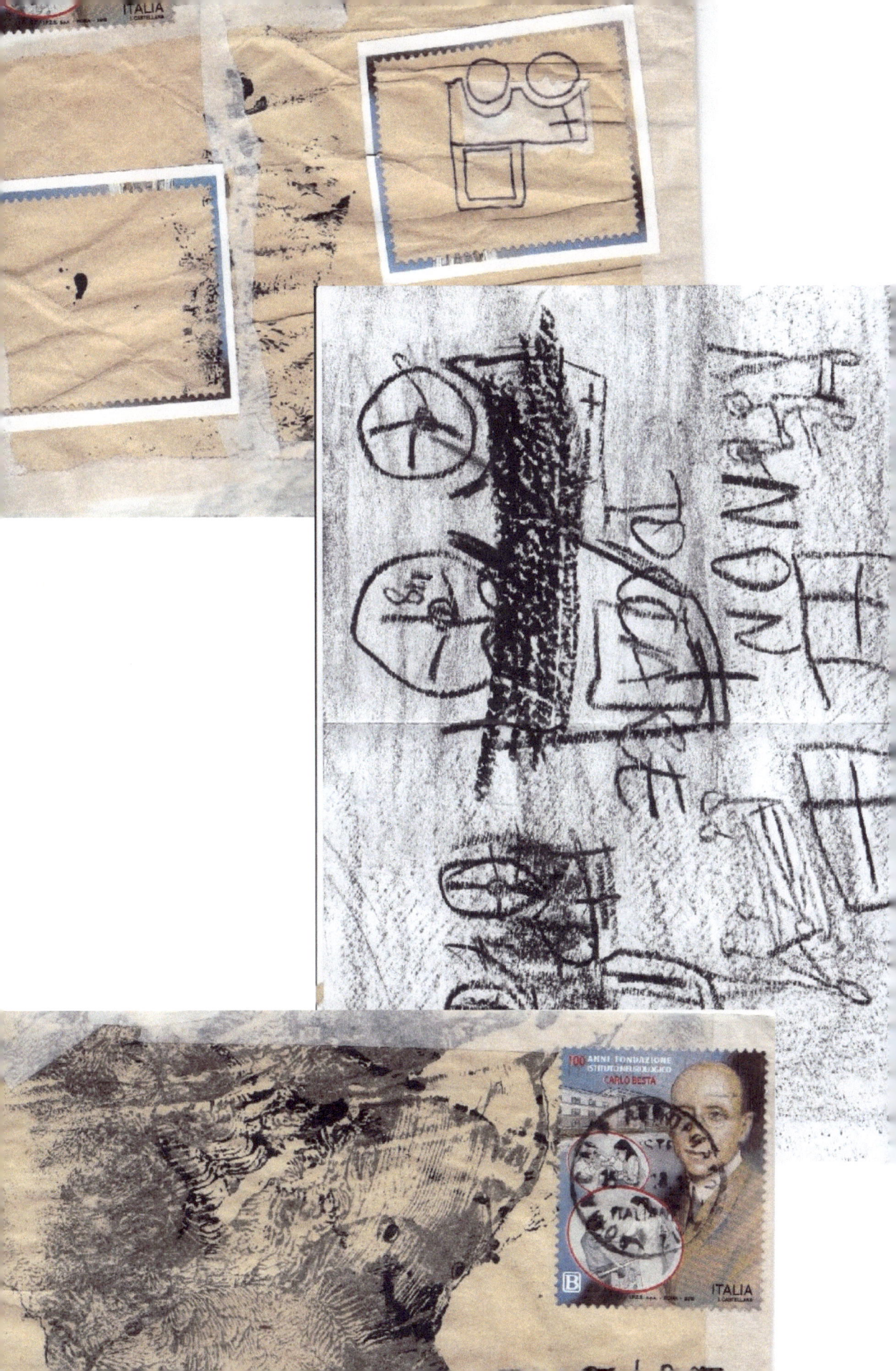

www.ingramcontent.com/pod-product-compliance
Lightning Source LLC
Chambersburg PA
CBHW041315180526
45172CB00004B/1103